STUDIES IN CREATIVE CRITICISM

Behind the Fourth Gospel

STUDIES IN CREATIVE CRITICISM

Behind the Fourth Gospel

BARNABAS LINDARS, S.S.F.

WIPF & STOCK · Eugene, Oregon

Wipf and Stock Publishers
199 W 8th Ave, Suite 3
Eugene, OR 97401

Behind the Fourth Gospel
By Lindars, Barnabas, S. S. F.
Copyright©1971 SPCK
ISBN 13: 978-1-60899-730-5
Publication date 6/8/2010
Previously published by SPCK, 1971

This Edition reprinted by Wipf and Stock Publishers
by arrangement with SPCK, London.

To V.T.B.S.

CONTENTS

PREFACE   9

1   THE RIDDLE OF THE FOURTH GOSPEL   11

2   THE SOURCES OF THE FOURTH GOSPEL   27

3   THE MAKING OF THE FOURTH GOSPEL   43

4   THE THEOLOGY OF THE FOURTH GOSPEL   61

NOTES   80

SOME BOOKS ON JOHN   83

PREFACE

In the spring of 1970 I was asked at rather short notice to undertake a main course of four lectures at the Vacation Term for Biblical Study in Oxford in the same year. I had recently completed the manuscript of a commentary on St John's Gospel for the revised edition of *The Century Bible*. I was therefore very glad of the opportunity to express some of the ideas which had taken shape in writing the commentary, and which had subsequently crystallized in my mind; and also to give some attention to current literature on John which had appeared since the manuscript was finished. It was also invigorating to be under the necessity of doing the work rapidly. The effort was rewarded by the response of the audience at the Vacation Term. It is at the request of a number of those who heard the lectures that I have prepared them for publication. The changes are very slight, though I have added brief analyses of John 6 and 13–20 which were not included in the original lectures.

In publishing these lectures I am aware that they contain numerous bold assertions for which far more supporting evidence is required than could be included even in this published form. This evidence will be given in the commentary to which I have referred, which I hope will be published early in 1972.

I would like to take this opportunity of expressing gratitude to Professor C. F. D. Moule, who read the manuscript, and to others who have made helpful comments and suggestions, especially Professor D. Moody Smith.

Above all my thanks are due to the committee and members of the Vacation Term for Biblical Study, who provided the stimulus for the work, and to whom this book is cordially dedicated.

Cambridge   BARNABAS LINDARS, s.s.f.
15th January 1971

9

1 THE RIDDLE OF THE FOURTH GOSPEL

The convention of starting with an apology is a necessity in the case of the Fourth Gospel. The literature on it is immense, and even a scholar who devotes all his time to the study of the New Testament cannot hope to keep up with it. The range of problems to which it gives rise is so large that it would take far more than the present four chapters to deal with them. We shall have to be severely selective, and restrict our aim to what can be accomplished in the limits of a short study. But the problems of St John's Gospel are too closely interrelated to allow a neat division into a few select topics. We shall inevitably touch many topics which cry out for further treatment, but which we shall have to refuse to follow up.

By choosing the title *Behind the Fourth Gospel* I have implied that it is possible to dig below the surface and to discover some at least of the sources which have been used by John. But this is a large assumption to make. What of the Gospel's own assertion that it is the work of an eye-witness? (21.24). What of the tradition that the author is none other than John the Apostle, who has hidden his identity behind the figure of the Beloved Disciple? It is not of course impossible that an eye-witness should use sources to refresh his memory, rather than write entirely out of his own head. But as soon as we turn to the work actually involved in uncovering sources, i.e. to the literary criticism of the Gospel, we meet the fact that 21.24 cannot sustain the theory to which it has given rise. For one thing it is found in the Appendix (ch. 21), which for various reasons must be held to be an addition made after the completion of the Gospel. For another, the hand of an editor is plain in the strange use of pronouns in this verse, which imply that the Christians responsible for publishing the Gospel identify the author with the Beloved Disciple, but do not imply the author's own word for it.

In this short study I will not discuss the case for the traditional authorship, though I will for convenience call the evangelist John. I will assume that the author was not the Beloved Disciple and was not an eye-witness of what he records, but was dependent upon the traditions which were available to him. These traditions may have been oral or written or both. I will moreover assume that the Gospel reached its final form some time in the last decade of the first century, which is the conventional date.

Other dates, both later (well into the second century) and earlier, have been suggested, but recent research has really precluded either of them. The John Rylands papyrus fragment (Pap. 52) is now dated not later than A.D. 130, which means that the Gospel was already circulating and being copied in Egypt by that date. On the other hand, the new emphasis on the Jewishness of the Gospel, with its striking community of ideas with the Dead Sea Scrolls, allows in principle a much earlier date in the first century. But this cannot do away with the indications within the Gospel itself that the point of final breach between Church and Synagogue has been reached. This is to be connected with the exclusion of the Minim and the Nazarenes from the synagogue (the twelfth of the Eighteen Benedictions).[1] This is dated about A.D. 85.

It may be noticed that I was careful to say "reached its final form" when I dated the Gospel in the 90s. It can well be that the Gospel was begun much earlier than this, perhaps in the early 80s. This is important, because it brings the date much closer to that of the Synoptic Gospels. It is quite probable that Luke was actually written later than John.[2] If so, it is relevant to our investigation, as there are significant links between Luke and John. If Luke is later than John, John cannot have borrowed from him, so that the connection must be explained along different lines. As far as Mark and Matthew are concerned, even though they were surely composed before John, the interval of time is not so great as to lead us to assume that John would have actually possessed them, even if he had had some kind of acquaintance with one or other of them. In fact it is likely that John had at least *seen* Mark, because (if we may assume the priority of Mark, though the issue is wide open again in contemporary scholarship) there are grounds for supposing that Mark was the originator of the Gospel *form*, which John also follows (i.e. the presentation of the kerygma in the form of a connected account of Jesus' ministry and teaching, combined with the passion narrative). But to say that John follows Mark's form is a very different thing from saying that he used Mark as his *source*.

Now I want to point out the consequence of the attempt to close the gap to some extent between the dates of the Synoptic Gospels and of John. As far as John's sources go, it suggests that his material was identical with, or parallel to, the sources used by the synoptists, rather than with the Synoptic Gospels themselves. Just as Synoptic criticism seeks to uncover the original items of tradition in order to work back to Jesus himself, so source-criticism of John may properly be undertaken with the saime aim. We ought to expect John to yield the same sort of results as the Synoptic Gospels when treated in the same way.

But this consequence only throws into sharper relief an entirely different one. It makes the unique character of John, its generally uniform and distinct style, and its advanced Christology—not to mention the presence of hellenistic ideas —all the harder to explain. There must have been considerable development between the collection of the underlying traditions and the use of them for the composition of the Fourth Gospel.

It is customary to express this development in terms of polemical aims. John is using the tradition to cope with new factors emerging in the Church. He is said to be opposing a docetic Christology (Hoskyns). Alternatively he is said to be supporting Christian claims to allegiance against those of the followers of John the Baptist (though the continuing existence of the Baptist sect at this date is far from certain). Or he may be attempting to cope with Jewish objections to Christianity, that the divine revelation of the Law of Moses is repudiated by Christians, and that they have raised Jesus to such a level that their worship of him and of God amounts to ditheism

(J. Louis Martyn).[3] Or we may take the older view that he is
concerned with internal problems of Christianity, such as the
delay of the Parousia and incipient gnosticism.

I do not wish to argue any of these positions in detail. I
simply mention them to draw attention to the profoundly
problematic character of John. Even if we agree on the one
hand that his sources are comparable to those of the Synoptic
Gospels, parallel to them if not actually identical with them,
we must on the other hand take into account the far-reaching
development of theology which the finished work comprises,
a development which goes hand in hand with the spread of
Christianity and its confrontation with new ideas and circumstances. We have to reckon with a many-sided process which
went on between the formation of the sources and the finishing
of the Gospel. By suggesting that the composition of the
Gospel was itself a fairly lengthy process, beginning in the
80s and not complete until the 90s, I am opening the possibility that something of this development may be discernible
within the composition of the Gospel itself.

Before we try to uncover the underlying sources, we ought
to look for signs of the complex process of the Gospel which
spans this period. The uniform style of John should not lead
us to jump to the conclusion that the work was undertaken at
a single sitting. There are, in fact, several factors which force
us to conclude that the Gospel is the product of a literary
process.

1. There are first of all the faulty connections, which can for
convenience be called the "aporias" of the Fourth Gospel
(*aporia*=perplexity). These are always seized on by source
critics as a sure sign of the redaction of documentary sources.
They may take several forms.

(*a*) There may be a *geographical* break, where Jesus appears
to be in the wrong place from the point of view of the sequence
of the narrative. The only obvious case of this is chapter 6,
where Jesus is in Galilee, though his departure from Jerusalem
is not mentioned (or at least implied) until 7.1. Hence it is

widely held that chapter 6 is misplaced. If so, we must reckon with literary confusion after the completion of the Gospel, rather than in the course of its construction. But there are other geographical aporias which are better concealed. Jesus is sometimes in Galilee and sometimes in Jerusalem. The episodes in each locality are complete in themselves, and there is no intrinsic reason why they should be given in the order in which they appear, apart from John's deeper interest in producing a theological progression of thought. Hence the notes of Jesus' movements are more or less artificial connecting links, which smooth over the geographical aporias. We may well conclude from this that John is making fresh use of already extant material.

(b) There are *temporal* aporias. Here we can think of the celebrated case of 7.21, where Jesus, back in Jerusalem after an interval of several months, refers to the healing miracle of chapter 5 as if it had happened only yesterday. Similarly, the allegory of the Good Shepherd (10.1–18) is taken up again in 10.27, in spite of the fact that verse 22 has indicated an entirely fresh occasion. Such features suggest that John has split up his source-material, in order to work it up into a more complex scheme.

(c) Then there are the *thematic* breaks. We are all familiar with the sudden intrusion of John the Baptist in the prologue (1.6–8). This may be very effective as a kind of foil to the main theme, but it is scarcely possible to believe that it belongs to the original form of the prologue.[4] A less obvious example is the introduction of the Paraclete in 14.16f, breaking the theme of Jesus' own return to the disciples and of their mutual indwelling with the Father. It is aporias like these which have led many critics to accept the theory of accidental displacements (e.g. Bernard, Bultmann). But even if this may account for some of the facts, it certainly cannot account for all. Nor do these critics make the mistake of supposing that they do so. But that the Gospel was subject to addition after it left its author's hands is plain for all to see in the Appendix (ch. 21).

There is no more glaring aporia that the new start at 21.1 after
the concluding comment of 20.30f.

2. A second approach to the literary process of John is to
subject the contents to the discipline of form-criticism. This
means classifying the contents according to distinct literary
types. The task may require some removal of editorial layers
before the correct classification of any given passage is brought
to light. The editorial work tends to obscure the distinctiveness
of the individual units by covering them with a monochrome
varnish, which blurs the colours. Only when the isolated units
have been uncovered is it possible to assess their value, either
as historical tradition or as theological assertions.

(a) One type of material can very readily be identified, and
that is the *editorial connections,* which I have already referred
to in speaking of the geographical aporias. These are the short
notes which tell us that Jesus went up to Jerusalem for a feast,
or that as a result of his teaching "many believed on him".

(b) The second is the *Synoptic-type narrative,* generally referred to as a pericope, like the Marriage at Cana or the Cleansing of the Temple in chapter 2. It is fairly obvious that these
are the pieces most likely to be fruitful for the recovery of
John's sources, especially as they sometimes afford opportunity
for word-by-word comparison with their Synoptic counter-
parts. Needless to say, from a strictly form-critical point of
view they need to be subdivided according to the various types
discerned in Synoptic study.

(c) By contrast with these pericopae, John is unique among
the Gospels in containing sustained *discourses,* whether in the
form of monologue, or consisting at least in part of dialogue.
The prologue (1.1–18) may perhaps be included under this
heading. Apart from that, the first discourse occurs in chapter
3, the conversation between Jesus and Nicodemus. Thereafter
this type of material forms the bulk of the Gospel up to and
including the Prayer of Jesus in chapter 17, though smaller
units of the same type even occur in the trial narrative and the

resurrection appearances. They are extremely difficult to analyse critically, and, as we shall see in a moment, represent the
point of greatest divergence in Johannine studies today.

(d) Besides these three types of material, which recur through-
out the Gospel, the passion narrative and resurrection appearances with which the Gospel closes are best left in a class by
themselves. The passion and resurrection narrative is, in a
sense, the Christian Passover Haggadah, and had its own separate history before being united with the other types of material
to form a fixed element of the Gospel form. John's passion
narrative shows a very clear debt to the fixed form which is
already apparent in the Synoptic Gospels. It is thus amenable
to comparative study in the same way as the Synoptic-type
narratives, which were our second type of material.

3. Before giving rather more detailed attention to these literary
types, I must mention a third approach to the literary process
of the composition of the Fourth Gospel. Again, this is not
something which excludes the other approaches, though inevitably it tends to complicate them. This is the test of consistency
with regard to content. If the Gospel exhibits irreconcilable
contradictions of fact or ideas, this may be evidence of more
than one hand. Fortna (whose book, *The Gospel of Signs,* we
shall be considering in the next chapter) lists in a footnote the
following elements which have been claimed to show ideological inconsistency in different parts of the Gospel: the
Beloved Disciple; Jesus' sonship, pre-existence, and heavenly
origin; "works" versus "signs"; messianism; ways of citing the
O.T.; eschatology; and the nature of faith (p. 16, n. 1). Most
of these can safely be set aside as the product of an over-subtle
criticism discovering distinctions where none exist. But the
question of eschatology bulks large in Bultmann's source analysis, and has given rise to much controversy. It is the question
whether references to consistent eschatology (the Jewish idea
of a future event which will close the present world order, and
in which the Son of man is the key figure) can be regarded as
stemming from the same hand as the numerous sayings about

eternal life, which appear to represent a timeless approach. As
both ideas occur in the discourses, which, as I have mentioned,
are very difficult to analyse, it can be argued that the discourses
have been composed originally from one point of view and
touched up to bring them into closer agreement with Christian
orthodoxy, which requires the other. Bultmann holds that the
timeless idea belongs to the core of the discourses, and the
consistent eschatology is the work of the editor. But on the
whole this ideological approach is too closely bound up with
subjective assessment of the worth of the material to yield
reliable results.

The effect of these various approaches to the literary character of John is to confirm the impression that the Gospel is the
end-product of a complex process. Some degree of alteration
after it left its author's hands is possible, but this cannot explain all the phenomena. The theory of accidental displacements accounts for only some of the difficulties. Moreover, the
proposed rearrangements always lead to further problems, so
that this theory is best discarded (so Barrett). Supplementation
after the completion of the Gospel is certain in the case of
chapter 21. But this is in fact good evidence for the compara-
tively sacrosanct character of the rest of the Gospel. For the
supplementer has not dared to insert his new material *before*
the original ending in 20.30f, which would have been the
natural thing to do.

We are left, however, with the four distinct types of material
separated on form-critical grounds, which belong to the weft
and woof of the Gospel, and these can be plausibly ascribed to
four different hands. In this way the character of the Gospel
as the product of a literary process can be explained along the
lines of source-criticism. This is in fact the theory of Bultmann
and his followers. Although his theory has not won acceptance
in British scholarship, it has had wide and lasting influence in
Germany. Even Bultmann's pupils, such as Bornkamm and
Käsemann, who in many respects differ from Bultmann himself, virtually take his source theory for granted. Moreover,
now that Bultmann's commentary has at last appeared in

an English translation, and now that some American scholars have taken up his ideas in recent work, we can safely predict that it will have more influence in this country than it has enjoyed so far. It is a theory which has very important consequences for the assessment of the Gospel as a whole.

According to this theory, the Synoptic-type narratives, the discourses, and the passion narrative are to be regarded as separate sources, each with its own internal history. The other distinct type (i.e. editorial connections) are assigned to the redactor of these sources, who also may be termed the evangelist.

1. The first type of material, the Synoptic-type narratives, consists mostly of the miracle stories in the first twelve chapters. On the basis of 2.11 ("This, the first of his signs, Jesus did at Cana of Galilee . . .") and 4.54 ("This was now the second sign that Jesus did . . ."), it is argued that there was a Signs Source (*Semeia-Quelle*), in which the miracles were enumerated. Most of the material in this source has close parallels with the Synoptic Gospels, though not so close as to suggest that it is simply a series of excepts from them. Also it contains some non-Synoptic items, such as the Marriage at Cana. Stylistically it has many semitisms, which point to a Palestinian provenance. Further characteristics will be mentioned in the next chapter, when I propose to consider two very recent reconstructions of this source in detail. The evangelist used this source for the narrative framework of the Gospel. Without it the Gospel would have presented more the nature of a treatise than a Gospel.

2. Secondly, we may mention the passion narrative, because of its similar character. Bultmann holds, as I think any source critic must, that John had access to a continuous narrative of the passion and resurrection, which was similar to the Synoptic accounts, but not identical with them. This also has its share of semitisms. Bultmann does not suppose that this was the same document as the Signs Source.

3. But it is the other remaining type, the discourses, which Bultmann separates as a Discourse Source (*Offenbarungs-reden-Quelle*) which is the most controversial feature of his theory. Here the most notable characteristic is the tension between a certain timeless idea of the revelation of God and the historic manifestation of this revelation in the person and work of Jesus. This tension is ascribed to the evangelist's re-working of his source for the purpose of his Gospel. The source begins with the prologue, which describes in measured and poetic verses the coming of the Revealer into the world, called here the Logos, or Word. In the discourses which follow the Revealer speaks in the first person. Using a series of self-revelation formulas, he declares himself to be the means of the world's salvation: I am the bread of life, I am the light of the world, I am the door, I am the good shepherd, I am the resurrection and the life, I am the way and the truth and the life. Moreover he describes his heavenly origin, which puts him into an altogether different category from the world of men: "I am from above, you are from beneath." "Before Abraham was, I am." Salvation consists in the possession of the divine knowledge: "Then you will know that I am he." "This is life eternal, that they may know thee, the only true God, and Jesus Christ whom thou hast sent." The language is that of hellenistic religion. The motif of the Revealer connects the source with the gnostic saviour-myth. The quasi-poetic form of the prologue, and the poetic character of many of the sayings in the rest of the discourses, suggest that the source was originally in the form of Semitic poetry. Bultmann argues that the source derives from a pre-Christian gnostic sect in Syria, where hellenistic and Semitic ideas had come together. The evangelist created the tension already mentioned by his attempt to identify the Revealer of the myth with the Jesus of history. His work is thus a Christianized form of gnosticism.

German scholars are in the habit of using in their books a variety of type-sizes to distinguish between the more important material and subsidiary matters. Anyone using Bultmann's commentary can quickly see, from this typographical feature alone, that he feels that it is this Christianized gnostic source which is the most important aspect of the Gospel. The evangelist is not interested in the facts of the life of Jesus, but only in the challenge to faith which he presents. In fact it was in his handling of the Johannine discourses that Bultmann first put forward his well-known programme of demythologization. The evangelist made this reinterpretation of a gnostic document the clue to his understanding of the Gospel tradition. Consequently the traditional material, i.e. the signs and the passion narrative, are subservient to the teaching of the discourses. The signs are not to be valued as history, but merely as symbols of the truth conveyed in the discourses. The evangelist has disclosed his aims not only in rewriting the Discourse Source to suit his Christian mould, but also in the editorial connections by which he has effected the redaction of the other sources. These connections draw attention to the reaction of faith on the part of Jesus' hearers, and it is precisely the evangelist's aim to produce faith. This becomes very clear in the words with which the Gospel ends (20.30f), though Bultmann holds that the evangelist has here simply reproduced the final words of the Signs Source with some slight expansion. He claims that the evangelist could use this conclusion of the older work for his own purpose without fear of misunderstanding on the part of the reader, because he has already made it clear what he means by "signs". They are "acts which speak" to the reader. It can even be argued from this final passage that the other editorial connections of a similar type have been modelled on this facet of the Signs Source, at the same time as radically reinterpreting it.

Finally, this brief presentation of Bultmann's theory would not be complete if I did not mention one other factor which may be held to pose a serious threat to his whole reconstruction. It is the fact that he is forced to assume that the discourses have been considerably disrupted by accidental displacements. He supposes that the original sheets of the evangelist's work got into hopeless disarray, and an ecclesiastical redactor did his best to sort them out into some sort of order, but was very far from being successful. This subsequent editor was to some extent guided by his own interests. He did not share the radical gnosticism of the evangelist, but was concerned to make the work presentable from an orthodox Christian point of view. Consequently he made some changes and additions to bring the work more into line with orthodox views. The references to the Son of man, which reflect a consistent eschatology, and the passage about the flesh and blood of the Son of man in chapter 6, with its obvious sacramental application, are due to his hand.

Bultmann's source criticism poses in the sharpest form the problem of the difference between the underlying sources and the finished product. The Signs Source bears a close relation to the earlier tradition. It is concrete in its outlook, and speaks of miracles as if they actually happened. It appears not to be concerned with the challenge to faith, with its demand to face the meaning of existence, which is involved in personal confrontation with Christ. To the evangelist, however, building on the gnostic material which lies behind the discourses, the whole meaning of existence is concentrated in the phenomenon of Christ. Even the miracle stories of the older tradition have no value, except as a means of leading to this confrontation and this existential demand. The point I want to make here is not that I necessarily agree or disagree with Bultmann's analysis, but that it illustrates very strikingly how our assessment of John is bound up with the theory we form about its origins. The effort to get behind the Fourth Gospel is not simply a literary-critical game, but an inescapable task in the process of discovering the real meaning of it in the form in which we know it.

But if I must commit myself one way or the other, I confess that I do not share the theory of Bultmann. It is not only that the complicated history of the formation and disruption of the discourses strains credulity. Nor is it an objection to the theory of a pre-Christian gnosticism in Syria, where such a production might have been inspired (though the possibility that such a gnosticism flourished is still open, it has yet to be shown that it could produce literary works such as this). My difficulty is that the theory presupposes too simple and rigid a distinction between the evangelist and his two main sources (Signs and Discourses). It is obvious that John uses traditional material in the narrative parts of his Gospel, both signs and passion story, so that in these parts it becomes fairly easy to discern the difference between the evangelist and his source. But I believe that even here the evangelist uses considerable freedom in handling this material, so that it is far from being a straight use of the source, but rather owes much to his creative writing. But when we come to the discourses the style becomes much more uniform. Bultmann does not rely on a separation of folklore elements and the evangelist's creative handling of them for his distinction between source and evangelist, but on a dogmatic criterion, the test of content. This is the most dubious of the three approaches to literary analysis of the Gospel which I outlined earlier. Ideas and phrases which accord with hellenistic and gnostic thought are isolated as the authentic substratum, whereas more specifically Christian ideas and phrases are taken to be superimposed by the evangelist. The process is exactly the reverse of what happened to the signs, which on Bultmann's view underwent a measure of hellenizing, whereas this material has been to some extent Christianized.

But when we look more closely at the discourses, we shall find that they too contain traditional material in the form of sayings of Jesus, which are just as much comparable to the Synoptic traditions as the signs. The criterion used to distinguish source and evangelist in the case of the signs works for the discourses too, though the element of underlying tradition is smaller and the amount of creative writing is very much greater. In spite of the high degree of uniformity in John's vocabulary and diction, which has been demonstrated by such scholars as Schweizer and Ruckstuhl, it is usually possible to isolate the traditional elements in the discourses. On the other hand, this uniformity must be taken seriously with regard to the creative writing. Apart from traditional Synoptic-type sayings embedded in them, the discourses do not show such a marked lack of inner consistency as to suggest the reworking of an extraneous source.

It is only fair that I should in conclusion give a concrete example of what I mean. Let us look at 8.12–20, a dialogue which begins with the saying "I am the light of the world". It is part of the highly complex and difficult discussion at the Feast of Tabernacles, which occupies the whole of chapters 7 and 8. Verse 12—on the light of the world—stands alone. Verses 13–20 do not follow from it very well. They are concerned with the issue of the proper witness to the truth and validity of Jesus' judgement. It is recognized by all scholars that this arises from the very similar discussion in chapter 5. There is a connection between verse 12 and the rest, however. This is the fact that John uses the theme of light, not simply with its expected connotation of spiritual illumination, but with the idea of showing up truth and falsehood. Thus it belongs closely with the theme of judgement and discernment. Bultmann transfers verse 12 to go with chapter 9, the Man Born Blind, where this theme of light is more extensively treated.

I do not want to challenge this at the moment, and we could really leave this verse out of account, except for the fact that it is a verse which shows clear dependence on the traditional, Synoptic-type, sayings of Jesus. And this is a fact which goes unrecognized in Bultmann's treatment of it. The relevant part of the verse reads: "He who follows me will not walk in darkness, but will have the light of life." The scope of the present study precludes detailed argument, so I must simply state baldly that I regard this as a reworking of an O.T. quotation with traditional sayings on discipleship. The quotation is Isa. 9.2: "The people who *walked in darkness* have seen a great *light*; those who dwelt in a land of deep *darkness*, on them has *light* shined." For the sayings on discipleship, compare Mark 10.28–30: "Peter began to say to him, 'Lo, we have left everything and *followed* you.' Jesus said, 'Truly, I say to you, there is no one who has left house or brothers. . . . who will not receive a hundredfold now in this time. . . . and in the age to come eternal life.' " Finally, "the light of the world" also occurs in a Synoptic saying (Matt. 5.14).[5]

The passage continues (verses 13–19) with the debate on the witness to Jesus. Bultmann assigns only the following to

the original discourse, before it was reshaped by the evangelist:
"Even if I do bear witness to myself, my testimony is true, for
I know whence I have come and whither I am going. Yet even
if I do judge, my judgement is true, for it is not I alone that
judge, but I and he who sent me. You know neither me nor my
Father; if you knew me, you would know my Father also." All
the rest has been added by the evangelist. It follows that not
only does the evangelist Christianize the source, but he also
turns it into a polemical discussion with the Jews. He interrupts
the source to make an argument which proceeds by logical
steps. The climax, that it is *the Father* who is the chief witness,
although the Jews do not know him, loses its force without
their contribution to the discussion, and the whole thing becomes a timeless statement of the close relation between the
Revealer and the Father in the act of judging. In spite of this,
however, the polemical tone remains, as Bultmann's nucleus
still retains the contrast between what "you" think and what
the Revealer declares.

But the other verses are not obviously in a different style,
and they add greatly to the effectiveness of the passage. Verse
13 complains that Jesus is witnessing to himself; the reply is
that his testimony has a different basis from what is usual in
human affairs. This is followed by a distinction between human
methods of judgement and his own. In verse 15 (omitted by
Bultmann) Jesus states that he does not judge men, i.e. according to human judicial procedure. Verse 16 modifies this by
explaining that he does nevertheless have an activity of judgement (the eschatological judgement is meant), but the procedure is comparable only to that of human judgement in so
far as the combination of his own and another's word of judgement corresponds with the Jewish requirement that there
should be the agreement of two witnesses. This is expressed
so cryptically that the next verse 17 (again omitted by Bultmann) is indispensable to make sense of the words. He can
then say explicitly in verse 18 that he and the Father are the
two witnesses which Jewish law requires. It is only at this
point that Jesus identifies the second witness as none other
than his Father, for in verse 16 he has only referred to him

vaguely as "him who sent me" (omit *pater* with Sin* Dsy[sc]).
Thus Jesus' answer in verse 19b ("if you knew me, you would
know my Father also") forms the grand climax, in which Jesus
expresses the complete unanimity between himself and the
Father. This is in fact the whole point of the argument.

It will be seen from this example that I regard Bultmann's
treatment of the passage as destructive of its real meaning and
based on false criteria. The attempt to isolate a pre-Johannine
Discourse Source is a most problematical undertaking. It is a
mistaken approach to the discourse element in the Gospel. I
will try to give a more positive approach in the third chapter
of this book. But the same criticism does not apply to the
material assigned to the Signs Source, where the use of old
material can be more clearly and more surely determined. Consequently our next step must be to examine the so-called Signs
Source. We must also give attention to the traditional material
which, as I have shown in conjunction with 8.12, is to be
detected in the discourses themselves. This will be the subject
of the next chapter.

2 THE SOURCES OF THE FOURTH GOSPEL

In our attempt to dig below the surface of the Fourth Gospel, we have examined four literary types of material which have been used as pointers to the composition of the Gospel. Two of these types stand together, the Synoptic-style narratives and the passion narrative. The other two types are the discourses and the editorial connections. Bultmann presupposed a pre-Johannine Discourse Source, which the evangelist not only united with the other material, but also reworked very heavily so as to make it applicable to the person of Jesus. We have seen reason to be very doubtful of this element of his source criticism. But the possibility of separating out the Synoptic-type material is much more promising. To say this is not to affirm the Signs Source postulated by Bultmann and his school, though this is one of the possible forms in which this material was available to John. In fact we can have a fairly wide range of views about this, stretching from the idea of a mass of mostly unrelated traditions, some of it written and some of it oral, to the opposite extreme of a single source, embracing not only the signs but also the passion narrative, in other words, a complete underlying Gospel. Bultmann, as we have seen, does not connect the Signs Source with the passion narrative. But he does include in it the main narrative elements of the first twelve chapters, including the call of the first disciples in 1.35–50 (though not the paragraphs on John the Baptist which precede this).

The theory of the Signs Source has won sufficiently wide acceptance to suggest that it could be brought within the scope of the kind of studies now popular in Synoptic criticism. The source, if reconstructed, could be subjected to form criticism. But as form criticism is atomistic, dealing with individual units, the Johannine material could be used without reconstructing it *in extenso*. But more recent Synoptic study has turned atten-

tion to redaction criticism, for example, the question why, if
Matthew was using Mark, he changed his source in the way
that he did, and what can be learnt from his changes about the
milieu in which he worked and the audience to which his
Gospel was addressed. If these questions are to be asked of the
Signs Source, and of John in his use of this source, it is obviously necessary that the effort should be made to reconstruct
it in detail. Thus the reconstruction of the Signs Source is due
to the impetus generated by the current interest in redaction
criticism.[1]

Seeing that this is the way N.T. studies are going, it is not
surprising that 1970 has seen the publication of two independent attempts to tackle the Signs Source from the point of view
of redaction criticism. The first to appear, though not the first
to be written, is an article by Jürgen Becker: "Wunder und
Christologie: zum literarkritischen und christologischen Problem der Wunder im Johannesevangelium".[2] The second is a
complete reconstruction of the source, which is held (contrary
to Bultmann) to include the passion narrative as well as the
signs, by the American scholar R. T. Fortna, entitled *The
Gospel of Signs: A Reconstruction of the Narrative Source
underlying the Fourth Gospel.*[3] The manuscript of this book
was completed before the end of 1968. Although Becker does
not provide a reconstruction of the text of the source, it is
clear from his article that he has not neglected to do this in his
study, though the limits of his article compel him to confine
himself to presenting the conclusions which can be drawn from
this labour. Fortna on the other hand is less concerned with the
results, and indeed his work is rather an exhaustive attempt to
establish just the text of the source as a basis for further
research.

On the whole there is a remarkable degree of agreement
between these two independent studies. Both agree against
Bultmann in assigning the witness of John the Baptist
(1.19–34) to the opening of the source. They then have the call
of the first disciples (1.35–50), which Bultmann had also included at the beginning of it. Both reconstructions then agree
that the source contained an orderly arrangement of miracle

stories, first those which are set in Galilee, and then those in
Jerusalem. But their reasons are slightly different. Becker is
faithful to Bultmann, and regards the composite passage 7.1–13
as containing an underlying stratum of tradition which belonged to the source, and which recorded Jesus' decision to
move from Galilee to Jerusalem. Fortna denies that any of this
passage belongs to the source, but assumes that the contents
were arranged in the form of a consistent geographical progress,
similar to the topographical arrangement of Mark.

Everyone knows that the main clue to the existence of the
source is the numbering of the first two signs, the Marriage at
Cana and the Healing of the Officer's Son. These, therefore,
have a fixed place at the beginning of the collection of signs
proper in both reconstructions. Thereafter the numbering
ceases, and there is room for difference of opinion on the order
of the rest within the broad topographical frame. Becker is not
concerned to define the exact order and limits of the source.
He contents himself with listing the signs in what seems to be
a natural order within this framework. So after the opening
sequence of the Baptist and the first disciples and the first two
numbered signs, he continues with the Feeding of the Five
Thousand and Walking on Water. Then the conversation of
Jesus with the woman of Samaria forms the transition to the
Judean section, which comprises the miracle at the Pool of
Bethesda, the Man Born Bind, and the Raising of Lazarus.

Fortna, however, tries to bring in as much of the narrative
material of the Fourth Gospel as possible into the source. He
holds that the numbering of signs continued. John let this feature stand in the first two cases, because he used them at the
end of a section. In all the other cases he had to drop it, because he was using the signs to lead into discourse. Incidentally,
I do not find this explanation convincing, as John is quite cap-
able of introducing a parenthetical note between sign and discourse when he wants to (e.g. the notes in 5.9b and 9.14 that
the cures were performed on the sabbath, neither of which is
assigned to the source by Fortna). But, following the suggestions of previous scholars, he puts in the Miraculous Catch
of Fish as the third sign, in spite of the fact that this piece is

only found in the Johannine Appendix, because it is said to be
the third resurrection appearance (21.14). You will see, then,
that he takes this story to have been originally an anecdote of
the ministry of Jesus, like its Synoptic counterpart in Luke 5.
He then has the Feeding miracle and Walking on Water, concluding the Galilean section. At this point the decision of Jesus
to go to Judea must be introduced. As he does not accept that
this is to be found in the substratum of 7.1–13, Fortna has the
ingenious idea that the deciding factor was the message of
Martha and Mary about the illness of Lazarus. So here he inserts the first part of this story. The conversation with the
woman of Samaria then takes place while Jesus is *en route* for
Bethany, and the raising of Lazarus is accomplished on arrival.
Then come the two miracles in Jerusalem, but Fortna places
the Man Born Blind before the Bethesda story, because it
happens while Jesus is on the road ("as he passed by", 9.1).

At this point the collection of signs is finished, and we should
expect the source to close with the summarizing verses, 20.30f,
which Bultmann had assigned to the source. This is how Becker
understands it. But not Fortna. He thinks that the source was
not just a book of signs, but a complete Gospel. He therefore
continues with the Cleansing of the Temple (from ch. 2), the
Priests' Plot to kill Jesus, the Anointing at Bethany, and the
Triumphal Entry. He assumes that the source had an account
of the Last Supper at this point, but this is the one passage
he does not attempt to reconstruct. Thereafter he has the Arrest
of Jesus, and the rest of the passion narrative including parts
of the resurrection narratives of chapter 20, ending with the
summary of 20.30f.

Fortna is well aware that his inclusion of the passion narrative will be less readily accepted than the rest of his reconstruction. But he claims to see sufficient continuity of style and
diction between the signs and the passion narrative to confirm
his impression that they belong together. What he does not
seem to realize is that in so doing he cuts the ground away from
one of the original arguments for the hypothesis of the Signs
Source itself. This was the observation that the use of "signs"
(*semeia*) in 20.30 is not suitable to the resurrection stories

which immediately precede it. This final summary does not
seem to take cognizance of the death and resurrection of Jesus,
but presupposes that his work consisted in the miraculous acts
which are designated *semeia* elsewhere in the Gospel. It could,
then, be the conclusion to a book of signs, but it can only be
the conclusion to the complete Gospel by straining somewhat
the natural sense of the words. Fortna is aware of this problem,
but he feels that somehow the strain is less if the earlier part of
the Gospel is a collection of signs, even though the passion
narrative occupies a good third of the reconstructed book, and
the word *semeia* never occurs in the course of it. Actually I am
inclined to agree with him that the verse can be quite reason-
ably understood as it stands, in spite of the lack of connection
with the passion and resurrection accounts. But it leads me to
the conclusion that we need not assign it to a pre-Johannine
stratum at all. Why should it not be John's own conclusion to
the Gospel?

Of the two reconstructions of the Signs Source, Fortna's is
clearly the more ambitious, and also the more open to criticism. Before considering the theology of the source and its significance for redaction criticism of the Fourth Gospel, which
is the really important matter, I should like to devote a little
more space to exposing the weaknesses of these reconstructions,
particularly that of Fortna. For Fortna is very insistent on the
necessity of sound method, and yet his case rests on large as-
sumptions which he appears not to question, and which I
regard as false.

1. His first assumption is that there could have existed a complete Gospel, containing quite a wide variety of material from
a form-critical point of view, which nevertheless did not contain any direct teaching of Jesus, apart from conversation within narrative. But parables and aphoristic sayings of Jesus were
available to John from some quarter, even if they were not
found in the narrative source. Dodd and others have shown
that many sayings of these kinds are embedded in the discourses, and we shall be looking at some of these in the next
chapter. The aphorisms include such a proverbial saying as

9.4: "We must work the works of him who sent me, while it
is day; night comes when no one can work". This is a particularly telling example, because it occurs, not in discourse, but in
the pericope of the Man Born Blind. Yet Fortna does not allow
it to be considered part of the story as it appears in the Signs
Source (quite rightly, in my opinion), but does admit that John
derived it from earlier tradition of some kind. This would lead
to the conclusion that John had a Sayings Source in addition
to the Signs Source. It would be something like the postulated
Q source, lying behind Matthew and Luke, which indeed does
include one miracle, but only one, and has no geographical
sequence or passion narrative. Another parallel would be the
gnostic *Gospel of Thomas*, which has no miracles at all. If we
are to start from the types of sources that are known to lie behind the Gospels, we could certainly assume such a Sayings
Source, and we could well accept a Signs Source in the sense
of a collection of miracle stories. And of course the passion
narrative is a special kind of source. What does seem unlikely
is that the Gospel form, such as was achieved by Mark, should
be reached simply by joining together a book of signs and a
passion narrative. For this we have no evidence at all.

Moreover, if it is true that miracle stories (Dibelius'
Novellen) constitute a special class of tradition, transmitted in
a different way from other material, it is most improbable that
it should contain the Witness of the Baptist and the Call of
the disciples at the beginning or the conversation with the
Samaritan woman in the middle. And if the Signs Source were
only a collection of signs, without necessarily including *all* the
signs which John makes use of, it would be just a very short
collection. It would then take its place alongside other short
collections, such as appear to lie behind the Synoptic Gospels,
like the controversy sequence in Mark 2. This would explain
why John has some numbered signs (actually only two), which
could well have belonged together in such a short collection.

2. The second assumption is that John is likely to have incor-
porated virtually the whole source in his Gospel, so that it can
be reconstructed simply by stripping off the non-Johannine

elements. Such a wholesale takeover of previous work is not impossible in principle, and indeed Matthew does just this with Mark. But John is on any showing a highly creative writer, so that such an idea is intrinsically improbable from the start. It is essential to examine his methods as a writer before trying to determine the extent of the source material which he has taken over untouched. In Fortna's reconstructed text of the source I see features which are characteristic of John ascribed to the source again and again. I can nearly always agree that, in any given pericope, John has reproduced quite a bit of the source verbatim. But he never does so completely. He always adapts the source to suit his own ends. He does this, not only by additional phrases of his own, but often by substituting his own rewriting for that of the source, sometimes recasting the story itself in the process.

Actually what John does is not dissimilar to Matthew. For Matthew is no mere scissors-and-paste man, but does creative adaptations of his own, as redaction criticism has shown. Matthew's example is instructive, because it is precisely in the miracle stories that he exercises the most freedom.[4] In a short chapter on the Stilling of the Storm, Bornkamm shows how Matthew has introduced light touches to make the story an object-lesson for disciples in time of danger. Similar motives are discovered by Held in his longer essay on "Matthew as Interpreter of the Miracle Stories".

In John's case it is especially in the dialogue that John's own creative hand is most clearly visible. We refer again, for example, to the Man Born Blind in chapter 9. Here Fortna retains as part of the source the leading question of the disciples in verse 2: "Rabbi, who sinned, this man or his parents, that he was born blind?" But obviously he cannot retain the reply of Jesus, that it was "that the works of God might be manifest in him", for that is so obviously Johannine. I have already remarked that the next verse, which contains a proverbial saying, has to be assigned to an extraneous source of Jesus' words. Again, Fortna's reconstruction of the Raising of Lazarus includes the greater part of 11.28–44, quite unaware of the extremely subtle way in which John uses the theme of the apparent grief of Jesus to build up to a breath-taking climax, as I hope to show in the next chapter.

This attribution of Johannine writing to the source appears at its worst in the story of the Samaritan woman, which of course contains no miracle and cannot be counted as one of the signs at all. Here a considerable amount of the Johannine discourse is regarded as belonging to the source. Fortna is not willing to admit that only the setting comes from a source, and that the entire conversation which depends on it derives from the evangelist. In fact the original story for which this was the setting is simply abandoned, and it is Fortna's determination to find *all* the source in John which makes him fall into this grievous error of ascribing the discourse to the source. This point really ties up with what I said just now about sayings of Jesus. For if the Signs Source can have the kind of conversation which is reproduced in chapter 4, it is surely likely that it would also have contained some of the truly Synoptic-type sayings as well.

The *coup de grâce* against the idea that the source should be recoverable almost in its entirety from the Gospel is in fact provided by Fortna himself. For of course he has actually included in it *one* sign which is definitely not found in the Gospel as it left John's hands, and that is the Miraculous Catch of Fish. For this belongs to the post-Johannine appendix (ch. 21). I do in fact agree with Fortna that the main body of chapter 21 is John's own composition, and that he has based it on a traditional story which also appears in variant form in Luke 5. But even so it is not part of the finished Gospel. It is an isolated extra which was only added to the Gospel after the evangelist's death. My own view is that John composed this piece after completing the Gospel in order to cope with a question which had arisen as a result of writing the Gospel, i.e. the question of the fate of the mysterious Beloved Disciple. The story is then used in an *ad hoc* production, and so falls outside John's planned scheme. This makes it very unlikely that John had the good fortune to have left out just one item of his source, which was the very thing to use when he subsequently had to write a bit more. This is a real case of the exception proving the rule.

In this case the rule, that all the source is contained in the Gospel, fails to pass the test. Becker was much wiser not to ascribe this story to the Signs Source, in spite of its possible connection with the numbering of the signs.

Enough has been said to shake confidence in the existence of the source as reconstructed, but we must still give it the benefit of the doubt, as we have yet to consider the theological implications of it. Here the shorter work of Becker is to my mind more acute than the longer work of Fortna. Both are agreed that the presentation of material in the source has a distinct slant from the point of view of Christology. There is a repeating pattern in the form of the signs, which appears at any rate in the Marriage at Cana, the Officer's Son, the Feeding of the Multitude, and the Raising of Lazarus, and may originally have applied to the others as well. In each case Jesus acts, not just out of compassion, but in order to manifest supernatural power, which demonstrates who he is. The titles applied to Jesus in the opening of the source (the witness of the Baptist and the first disciples) define him as the Messiah or the prophet or the Son of God. Becker argues that the last two of these are the important ones, and connects them with the *theios anēr*, the man from heaven, of the hellenistic saviour-myth. Each sign thus constitutes an epiphany of the divine man. At the conclusion the source notes that the people believed in Jesus as a result of his signs. Hence the main purpose of the source is to compel belief in Jesus as the heaven-sent saviour by the sheer impressiveness of his miraculous deeds. It is thus not surprising that a recurring feature of the source is the heightening of the miraculous element in the traditions contained in the source. Thus the paralytic at Bethesda has already suffered thirty-eight years, the blind man has been blind from birth, and Lazarus has been dead four days.

On this showing the source has a well-defined purpose, to produce faith, and a very restricted range of reference, as there is no other interest apart from this Christology. There is a total absence of other items of interest to primitive Christianity, which one would suppose would be bound to show through somewhere. Even though he includes the passion narrative,

Fortna says that the Spirit (apart from the messianic anointing of Jesus himself), the Church, the sacraments, ethics, and ideas of salvation, forgiveness, and grace "find no place in it, or only passing mention". He should also add that there is no word about the passion, apart from the passion narrative. Whereas Q has sayings on discipleship which bring in the cross, and Mark has the passion predictions and various other references to the passion, the source apparently betrays not a hint of suffering either for Jesus or for the disciples before the passion narrative is reached. Moreover, the source nowhere uses the title Son of man, nor refers to the filial relationship between Jesus and God. There is no explicit eschatology or conventional apocalyptic language. All these are things which enter the Gospel only through John's own work of composition. His ideas on these subjects are derived, no doubt, from the living tradition within his Church, but certainly not from the source. One cannot help feeling even more sceptical about the whole reconstruction when so much of what is common to all the early Christian literature is missing from the source. The catalogue of negations is almost the last word of Fortna on the source, and it is not a happy note on which to finish the book.

Becker, however, is primarily interested in the source, not for what it was in itself, but for what John was intending to do by contrast with it. He says that John accepts the basic character of the source, the heightening of the miraculous, the miracles as signs of the *theios anēr,* the emphasis on belief which these evoke. But the evangelist brings this picture of a wonder-worker among men into the larger cosmic frame of late Jewish dualism, the primeval struggle between light and darkness, in which Jesus is the chief actor. John introduces the theme of the passion as the crucial moment in this drama. Becker frankly describes the source as docetic, because of its omission of the passion and its picture of Jesus as a *theios anēr.* He says that John is concerned to correct this docetism. Hence the response to the signs becomes in his treatment of them more equivocal and problematic. They not only produce faith but also arouse opposition. Consequently the signs, without losing their form as epiphanies, produce the crisis, the moment of decision, out of which men may rise to the quality of faith required for participation in eternal life. In the last resort the signs are really unnecessary to faith, once the Christology to which they point has been appropriated. For Jesus is himself the gift of which he is the giver. He gives the bread of life, but he *is* the bread of life (6.35). The great "I am" sayings provide the Johannine meaning of the signs. But though the believer can do without the signs once he has reached faith of this kind, this does not mean that the signs are not meant to be regarded as historical. Becker is resolutely opposed to Käsemann's contention that John was himself a docetist.[5] The events of the Gospel, including the resurrection, really happened, and they happened in the flesh of Jesus Christ. But the point is that men must not stop at the flesh. If they do so, they will only be scandalized, failing to reach the eternal life which has been promised. Only if they pass beyond it to the revelation of which it is the vehicle, can they participate in the true object of the incarnate life of Jesus. Having reached that end, they no longer need the flesh. The risen Christ no longer needs to be seen.

There is a great deal of truth in all this. I do not want to join issue with Becker over his sketch of the evangelist's theology. But I find myself far from happy about his idea of the relation of it to the source. It seems to me very strange that John should take over a source, fully approving of its rather special character as an appeal to wonder, and yet at the same time should make it the major purpose of his own work to subject the source to a radical criticism. The Fourth Gospel is pre-eminently an evangelistic work, very positive in its aim. We should always be wary of crediting John with polemical aims against other contemporary presentations of Christianity. Why reproduce verbatim a source which is so grievously inadequate? Why not simply rewrite it, if it must be used for lack of other sources, in such a way as to make the whole Gospel speak with one mind?

When we look carefully at the relation between the extraordinarily limited theology of the source and the wide spectrum of John's magnificent theology, a new point emerges. John opposes the views of his source, not by directly contradicting them, but by bringing them into a fuller context which puts them into a new light. Thus the source shows Jesus the wonder-worker producing faith; John shows Jesus, the Word of God, doing wonders which are the works of God, producing a crisis of decision which leads either to rejection of Jesus, and so of God, or to faith in him which opens the way to eternal life in fellowship with Jesus and God. The second is not opposed to the first, but it is the same as the first plus a good deal more. In other words the theology of the source is a pale ghost of John himself. The reconstruction of the Signs Source has not recovered an authentic independent document, but it is really a filter whereby the Gospel of many colours has all the colours cut out except one. No wonder it gives such a distorted impression.

If we are to reject the theory of the Signs Source, what, then, are we to put in its place? Certainly something more complex. We have seen enough to realize the danger of over-simplification. But we have also seen, in the course of the extended criticism of the theory, some lines which may direct our search.

1. First, if it is a mistake to suppose that the traditional material in John comes from a single source; the only other alternatives are that it came from a mass of unrelated traditions or from several short collections (or perhaps both: some short collections and some individual items). As there is evidence that short collections lie behind the Synoptic Gospels, it is reasonable to suppose that the same holds good of John. It is obvious that no single theological tendency is likely to unite this assortment of material before John imposes his own pattern on it all. This is not to deny that some of the collections may have had their own tendency.

2. The passion narrative is a special case, the earliest form of continuous narration, comprising a sequence of episodes in more or less fixed order. Bultmann and Becker are well justified

in refusing to regard this as part of the same source as the signs.

3. The numbered signs certainly suggest the nature of one of the other short collections. Its character is indicated by the Marriage at Cana, the first item in the collection, which does indeed show the tendency to treat miracle as epiphany. But we only know for certain of one other item, the Officer's Son, and this has been more extensively recast by John and so shows less of the character of the source. We have no warrant to assume that this collection included the Baptist and the call of the first disciples, which have such an important place in both Becker's and Fortna's estimate of the theology of the Signs Source. This collection is known to have contained two Galilean traditions, and may have had more. But it is a gratuitous assumption that it also contained the Jerusalem traditions, or had geographical arrangement of its content.

4. If the pale ghost of John is not to be traced to the underlying collections, we must assume that it belongs to the manner in which he handles his material, i.e. he dresses up the individual pericopae as ghosts of himself, before presenting himself in more substantial form in his more creative writing which follows them. To put it more plainly, John himself retells the miracles in the manner of an epiphany in order to lead into the crisis of decision which really interests him. In the discourses, as all commentators recognize, John frequently advances his argument by way of naive misunderstanding. This opens the way for finer distinctions of meaning and deeper analysis of the point at issue. A classic example is the Samaritan woman, who takes Jesus' offer of "living water" to refer to a perpetually running stream, before the spiritual meaning is brought to light. Now the function of the miracle stories in John is rather similar to this. The impression that Jesus is a wonder-worker is intentional at the stage in the argument to which they belong, i.e. the opening of it. It cannot be taken for granted that, before John rewrote them, they would have given this impression. Only strictly narrative details can be attributed to the sources,

and the element of dialogue in them is always coloured by John's rewriting. Of course John's adaptation of his material extends to many narrative details as well.

5. Similarly John is also probably himself responsible for some degree of fusion of similar but originally distinct stories which were available to him. These may have been in different collections, from which he has selected only what he found needful. The fusions could, of course, have happened already in his sources, but the possibility that they are due to John himself should at least be kept open. I give two examples.

(a) The healing of the paralytic at the pool of Bethesda (5.1–9) is a Jerusalem story unknown to the Synoptic tradition. But it has been fused with the well-known Galilean story of the man who was let down through the roof, so that the final instructions, "Take up your pallet and walk", are verbally identical with that tradition (Mark 2.1–12). But this is not the end of the fusion. For John adds for good measure the detail that the miracle took place on the Sabbath. This is a feature of other stories in the short collection contained in Mark 2.1—3.7, but not of this particular one. I doubt if any of the elements of the resulting story come from the collection of the numbered signs.

(b) The other example is the Anointing at Bethany (12.1–8). This is a fusion of the Bethany story of the anointing of Jesus' head, which is found in the early part of the passion narrative in both Matthew and Mark, with a Galilean story of the washing of Jesus' feet with the woman's tears, found only in Luke 7. Luke's very elaborate version of the story has been influenced by the Bethany story, which he omits from the passion narrative. John, on the other hand, knows none of Luke's elaborations, but has drawn some details from the Galilean story in his retelling of the Bethany story. It is clear that John is not dependent on Luke as such, but on a source independently used by Luke. Presumably John had the Bethany story in the source of his passion narrative.

It is evident from these examples that John uses only bits and pieces of his source material, so that reconstruction in full is an impossible undertaking. In the case of the Jerusalem story of the healing at Bethesda, we cannot tell how it ended originally because John has replaced the ending with the Galilean story.

6. We must not forget that John also had at his disposal a number of sayings and parables of Jesus, which may have belonged to one or more short collections, or have been included in some of the collections from which he has drawn his narratives, or have existed independently as floating items of tradition. The analogy of what John has done with the signs suggests that the discourses in which these are found are John's own compositions, in which he has used the sayings as the basis for very far-reaching creative developments. Just as the signs are traditional stories reworked by John for the purpose of his Gospel, so the discourses are traditional sayings expanded and developed with the same aim in view. It is not necessary to postulate an extraneous Discourse Source, which has been given a Christian veneer by means of the addition of some sayings of Jesus and a wholesale theological recasting. We have noticed that, whereas Becker is confident about the existence of the Signs Source, he does not accept the theory of the Discourse Source. In fact it is precisely the discourses, embodying the full expression of John's themes, which enable Becker to contrast the theology of John with that of the Signs Source, and even to assert that he is consciously correcting it.

7. Finally, it is a mistake to distinguish rigidly between narrative and discourse in John. It is obvious in the case of the long account of the Raising of Lazarus in chapter 11 that the two types have there completely merged. John builds up his longer narratives in just the same way as he builds up his discourses. So the Witness of the Baptist and Call of the First Disciples in 1.19–51 is a kind of acted discourse, as I hope to show in the next chapter. It is based on traditional items, but it has been creatively handled for John's purpose of showing who Jesus is. We can understand much better how John achieves his object, if we read it after first analysing an extended dis-

course. When we know John's habits as a literary craftsman, we are in a better position to assess his treatment of narrative, where traditional material bulks larger. We shall then be saved from the trap of thinking that John's narrative is an almost straight reproduction of a source, only lightly touched up. In fact his source or sources in 1.19–51 lie very much in the background. On the basis of them he has created an entirely new composition. Hence the first thing that must be done is to study John's technique as a writer. Only when this is done shall we be in a position to estimate his use of sources on the one hand, and his methods of combining narrative and discourse into the larger whole of the complete Gospel on the other. The result will, as it turns out, go some way to solving the problems of aporias in John which we observed in the first chapter of this book. So in our next chapter we shall start with some examination of John's literary technique, and see where this takes us in our attempt to solve the riddle of the Fourth Gospel.

3 THE MAKING OF THE FOURTH GOSPEL

Our study of the sources of the Fourth Gospel has shown reason to doubt the existence of the Discourse Source, as postulated by Bultmann, and the impossibility of reconstructing an extended Signs Source, or Gospel of Signs. The theology which the latter is supposed to have carried is really only an abstraction from the theology of the Gospel as a whole, what I have called a pale ghost of John himself. The conclusion was reached that John's handling of sources can be properly assessed only if attention is first paid to his methods as a writer. For this purpose we need not concern ourselves with the finer details of his Greek vocabulary and diction, which have been fully investigated by Schweizer and Ruckstuhl. It is sufficient to look at the form and structure of some representative passages. These need to be complete in themselves, without raising the problems of aporia which so greatly complicate the question of the composition of the Gospel as a whole. But they need to be long enough to reveal John's aims and methods.

I want to plunge straight into the deep end and take a discourse which may seem a surprising and daring choice. It is the dialogue between Jesus and the Jews which ends with the immensely impressive claim, "Before Abraham was, I am!" (8.31–58). In fact, before we even begin to look at it, we have identified one of John's literary characteristics, his ability to build up his material to a climax which makes a powerful emotional impact. It is this capacity for emotional effects which is so important for understanding John, and which seems to me to be so often neglected by students of the Fourth Gospel. But we must go back to the beginning of the discourse in 8.31 to find out how John reaches this climax.

The piece begins with the statement that the disciples of Jesus will know the truth and consequently be free.[1] This implies that otherwise they would be in bondage, and the Jews

complain that, as descendants of Abraham, they are free in any
case. Here already we can realize that John is dealing with a
living dispute between Christians and Jews, which is very similar to the issues which faced Paul in his struggle with the
Judaizing element in the Church. But we must not stop over
that, for we are here concerned with the literary characteristics.
And the thing to notice about this opening dialogue in verses
31 to 33 is that it is really rather artificially contrived. John is
laying out the themes of the discourse—truth, freedom, bondage, ethnic and spiritual descent.

It is not until the next verse (34) that we reach the real
foundation of the argument, to which the preceding verses have
been the prelude. The solemn opening, "Amen, amen, I say to
you", is not just a stylistic trick. It is a recurring sign that John
is making use of a saying of Jesus from his stock of traditional
material. But in fact this verse does not actually give the underlying saying, but rather one side of John's application of it. The
actual saying is a parable contained in verse 35, the Parable of
the Slave and the Son. Following Semitic usage, we should
understand the definite article as a generic usage, and translate:
"A slave does not continue in a house permanently; a son continues permanently", i.e. as the possessor of an inalienable right
of inheritance. Both Dodd and Jeremias recognize in this verse
a parable of Jesus. John does not want to follow up the contrast
between slave and son, and that is why he deals with the slave
in verse 34, before giving the parable itself.[2] He wants to deal
primarily with the son, because the purpose of using this parable is to put the point that Jesus actually is in the position to
give a share in a perpetual inheritance, which is his of right.

From this point the discourse is concerned with the question
of the identity of the son in the parable. Is it the Jews or is it
Jesus and his disciples? The matter is complicated by the fact
that the father has not yet been determined. The Jews have
claimed descent from Abraham, but Jesus (disregarding his
own Jewish descent on the human plane) asserts that he too has
a significant father. It is important to realize that in verse 38
Jesus does not actually say who his father is. There was no
capital F in the original Greek! Moreover, Jesus at once

queries the Jews' claim to be sons of Abraham. He suggests that they really have a different father, again not revealing who he means. Then he shows that his own Father is none other than God, which explains why he speaks the truth. The Jews, seeing the way the argument is going, abandon the claim to be sons of Abraham, and claim themselves to be sons of God—but only to be told that they are just the opposite, sons of the devil, who is the father of lies and the opponent of the truth. Here we may note how, beginning artlessly from a simple parable, John has drawn out the issue to form a startling black-and-white contrast. And we should also take note of another feature, his delaying tactics, the way he holds back first the identity of Jesus' Father, then the identity of the Jews' real father, so that realization of the truth comes gradually and with all the greater effectiveness.

At verse 48 there is a break in the argument. What is John going to do next? He has not come to the end of what he has to say, for he has not yet shown what it is to be free in the Father's house. So John changes the subject by bringing in the suggestion of the Jews that Jesus is mad, himself spirit-possessed, which ironically is nearer the truth of their own situation, as men under the domination of the devil. But this is only the lead-in for the new theme. And the point to notice about this is that John now takes up a fresh aspect of the parable of verse 35, which has not so far been brought into the discussion. This is the idea of permanence: "The son continues for ever". Here we have a recurring feature of John's literary technique. He takes up the points of his basic statement successively, going back to the beginning to pick up a fresh point, but expounding it in the light of what he has already said in expounding earlier points. In this case he expresses the idea of continuing for ever in the phrase "he will never see death" (verse 51; "taste death", verse 52). Again we have the "Amen" opening, and this alerts us to look for another traditional saying of Jesus. Sure enough we have it in the Synoptic tradition: "Amen, I say to you, there are some standing here who will not taste death before they see the Son of man coming in his kingdom" (Matt. 16.28; cf. Mark 9.1). Characteristically

the Jews take Jesus' words literally. They complain that even
Abraham and other holy men like the prophets could not
escape death (verse 53). We notice in passing how John is careful not to lose Abraham from the argument, in spite of verses
41 to 44. The literalism of the Jews' response paves the way
for the crucial question "Who do you claim to be?"

For answer Jesus first recapitulates the argument of the
preceding section. He is the Son of the Father, and therefore
possesses the truth. Then he says that even Abraham was well
aware of this, and indeed is now, for he lives in paradise according to popular belief (cf. the parable of Dives and Lazarus,
Luke 16.19–31). Alternatively, the reference here may be to
another popular idea, preserved in rabbinic sources, that Abraham was granted a vision of the future course of history which
would be the consequence of the birth of Isaac. Whichever of
these is operative here, John contrives to make it sound as if
Abraham and Jesus are contemporaries. And of course the
Jews once more miss his meaning by taking the words too
literally. If Abraham saw Jesus' day, then presumably the reverse is true, and Jesus has seen Abraham. This gives the cue
for the grand finale: "Amen, amen, I say to you, before Abraham was (i.e. was born or came into being), I am." It is the lack
of concord between the two verbs which give this its startling
effect. It does not seem possible to identify another saying from
the tradition here, in spite of the "Amen" opening, which has
been used, then, for the sake of effect. It is probably wrong to
assume that the "I am" is intended to recall the divine name
of Exod. 3.14. It is rather an allusion to the self-predication of
the Wisdom of God (cf. Prov. 8.27, MT). All the "I am"
sayings in John are best understood in terms of a Wisdom
Christology, which also lies behind the Logos doctrine of the
Prologue.

However, we must not stop over this. In any case this discourse raises large issues which it would be fascinating to pur-
sue further, if there were space. But we have limited our aim
to a study of John's methods as a writer The passage has shown
John's use of traditional sayings, the way he builds up his argument by way of formal exposition of a saying, exposing it

phrase by phrase, the delaying tactics whereby the points come over with greater effectiveness, the trick of literal misunderstanding, and above all the emotional impact of a carefully prepared climax. These are not merely the habits of a writer. They are much more the methods of a preacher. Although the discourse is in substance a disputation with the Jews,[3] the form is really that of homiletic, in which the element of emotional effect is just as important as the logic of the argument. This gives a prima facie case for the supposition that the Fourth Gospel began life as separate homilies, which John subsequently used as the basis for a continuous Gospel. The discourse is, then, not a report of an actual debate, in which Jesus performs the function of the Christian protagonist.[4] It is rather a sermon addressed to the Christians in order to deepen and strengthen their faith in a situation where Jewish objections to Christianity are a matter of vital concern.

With these factors in mind, I want next to look at an example of the combination of sign and discourse, so as to see how John makes use of narrative traditions. Again it will be advisable to take a piece that is complete in itself, uncomplicated by the problem of aporias. Hence we now turn to chapter 6, which contains the great discourse on the Bread of Life. The chapter consists of two miracles, the Feeding of the Multitude and the Walking on the Water, followed by the long discourse, and ending with the effects of it upon the hearers and upon the disciples themselves. The two miracles obviously already stood together in the underlying tradition, as we can easily see from the Synoptic Gospels. We must not stop to see how John has handled these, but confine our attention to the discourse itself. Here we find the same characteristics as we found in chapter 8. It begins with an "Amen" saying in verse 26. This is an adaptation of a saying which actually occurs in the context of one of the Synoptic parallels of the feeding miracle, Mark 8.11f: "The Pharisees came . . . seeking from him a sign from heaven. And he . . .said, 'Why does this generation seek a sign? Amen, I say to you, no sign shall be given to this generation.' " This has been adapted to apply to the theme of eating, and the reason for this eventually appears in verse 31: "He gave them bread from heaven to eat". This is a quotation from the manna story (Exod. 16.4).[5] Thereafter the whole of the discourse is an exposition of this text, in which Jesus shows himself to be the true bread from heaven, which is the real food for the soul. The successive stages of the argument keep reverting to the text, defining it afresh, until all its implications are exhausted.

Thus the exposition begins with consideration of the *gift* of the heavenly bread (verses 32–40). We notice that this is introduced by another "Amen" saying (verse 32). Again it is based on the Jesus-tradition, for it carries an unmistakable echo of the Lord's Prayer. This is clearer still when the words are repeated in verse 34: "Give us this bread always".[6] It is further expanded with an "I am" saying which is clearly based on the Jewish Wisdom tradition (verse 35; cf. Sir. 24.21 and Prov. 9.5). Jesus, as the bread from heaven, is like the Wisdom of God, which enters into the souls of men, and he provides a comparable and more lasting satisfaction. This continuing effect is expressed in terms of consistent eschatology in the remainder of the paragraph (verses 37–40).

The next stage in the discourse characteristically reverts to the opening text, but takes up the development of it which has already been given in the preceding verses. So the words "I am the bread which came down from heaven" in verse 41 constitute a form of the quotation in verse 31 with modifications derived from verses 33 and 35. The objections of the Jews at this point form another example of John's technique of proceeding by way of an over-literal interpretation. The exposition is now concerned with the *nature* of the heavenly gift. It is the true Wisdom, the true teaching of God (verse 45 = Isa. 54.13), by contrast with the manna in the wilderness, which was merely food for the body. The contrast conceals another, which is more directly related to the situation of John and his readers. For John here draws on Jewish exegesis, in which the miracle of the manna was interpreted as a sign of the gift of the Law, which is the Wisdom of God.[7] The Law is superseded by Jesus, just as the manna was superseded by the Law. It follows that, whereas the former gift could never have lasting effects, the present gift is of such a kind as to lead to eternal life (verses 49–51).

Finally, the exposition turns to the most controversial and striking feature of all. The note of strife with which the paragraph begins helps to heighten the emotional tension. The words used in this verse (52) are linked to the original quotation of verse 31 by the phrase "to eat". In the next verse yet another "Amen" saying lays out the point at issue in terms of further items from the Jesus tradition. It is an amalgamation of a saying comparable to Matt. 18.3 (cf. John 3.3) with the well-known eucharistic words of Jesus at the Last Supper. It has already been pointed out that to receive Jesus as the bread from heaven satisfies not only hunger but also thirst (verse 35). So the lines are already set to express this in terms of the flesh and blood of Jesus in the Eucharist. But the point of this stage in the exposition is nothing so parochial as an exhortation to attend Holy Communion. To John the flesh and blood of Jesus refer to his passion. The whole point is that it is *Jesus crucified* who is the gift of God for the life of the world. Only when men accept and assimilate Jesus incarnate, crucified, and risen, are they in a position to have eternal life—or, as John puts it at the end (dropping all the symbolism and speaking in straight terms of personal relationship), are they in a position to abide in him with the Father for ever.

Many scholars have argued that this last section, on eating the flesh of the Son of man, is not an original part of the discourse. But I cannot agree with this, for it is the climax to which all the rest has been leading. As the bread of life, Jesus is not merely the divine Wisdom by which "they shall all be taught by God" (verse 45), but the one who was made man and died on the cross for the life of the world.

All this has given us only another example of the literary method which we have already seen in chapter 8. But what I want to emphasize is the fact that the connection of the discourse with the preceding sign of the Feeding of the Multitude is really very thin. The real basis of the discourse is the text from the manna tradition, and not the feeding miracle at all. This text performs the same function as the parable of the

Slave and the Son in 8.35. But the feeding miracle has an obvious connection of theme. Hence we can now see that John has used it, not as the basis of the discourse, but as an introduction to it. John secures the interest of his hearers by telling a story of Jesus. He then carefully correlates an associated saying from the tradition with the actual text of the homily. The homily could have had an independent existence before John decided to introduce it with the sign. But even with the sign at the beginning, the chapter as a whole could have existed as an independent piece, before being taken into the sequence of the Gospel.

Now let us turn back to chapter 5, where we have a similar case of sign and discourse. But this time we are going to be faced with the problem of continuity, of its relation to the larger plan of the Gospel. The sign is the healing of the paralysed man at Bethesda. I have already shown that this is a fusion of a Jerusalem story with the Galilean pericope of the man let down through the roof, and also that it has a further extraneous feature in the note that the cure was performed on the Sabbath. This feature plays a vital part in the structure of the chapter as a whole, as it provides the issue which bridges the transition from the sign to the discourse. This is the claim of Jesus to hold a position which gives him the right to set aside the Sabbath. He justifies this on the grounds of the special relationship between his acts and the work of God himself (verse 17). This is the starting-point for the discourse.

But when we look at it we find once more that it is not at all based on the sign, but has its own text in the shape of another traditional saying of Jesus with "Amen" opening. Here again a parable has been identified independently by Dodd and Gächter in verse 19 (where again the article must be read as "a" and the capital letters dropped). It is the parable of the Apprenticed Son: "A son can do nothing of his own accord, but only what he sees his father doing; for whatever he does, his son does likewise". The discourse continues as an exposition of this saying, using the same techniques as we have seen elsewhere, and I will not go on to analyse it. I simply want to point out that the relation of the miracle to the discourse is so slight that it could be effected only by adding to the story the issue of the Sabbath. But then this issue appears to play no part in the discourse either.

But that is not quite the case, because we now come to a new feature of John's methods. For there is a further reference to the sign and also to the issue of the Sabbath in a short piece of dialogue, which purports to belong to an entirely separate occasion, i.e. 7.16–24. This is one of the most striking cases of aporia in the Gospel. Naturally attempts have been made to overcome the difficulty by supposing that the original order of the composition has been interfered with. In any case chapter 6 does not belong between chapters 5 and 7. But my own view is that John intended the order of material to be like this, and that he had definite reasons for constructing it in this way. I regard 7.16–24 as an item of the discourse of chapter 5 which has been deliberately held over to form the starting-point for the complex debates which occupy chapters 7 and 8. True to type, 7.16 begins the section with an allusion to the parable of 5.19, but also in words reminiscent of the beginning of an intermediate section at 5.30. The whole section completes the indictment of the Jews, which has been so large an issue in the discourse of chapter 5.

Here, then, is a further aspect of John's technique, the device of holding over part of his materials for a later occasion. Obviously this cannot have been a feature of them in their first phase as independent homilies. It is not what John does as a preacher, but it is one of his methods as a writer, when he adapts his homilies to make the Gospel. One answer, then, to the problem of aporias in John is that John is putting together existing separate pieces, and sometimes maintains continuity by the use of overlap between one piece and the next.

Of course this observation would not be convincing on the basis of one passage alone. But in fact we have another very similar example in the Shepherd allegory of chapter 10. This consists of the parable (or rather fusion of two parables, as argued by J. A. T. Robinson[8]) in 10.1–5. Then the rest of the piece is an exposition of the parable, following John's usual technique. Hence the allegory does not present a unified picture, but takes up each point of the parables successively, gradually reaching the climax in the statement that the Good Shepherd makes a voluntary sacrifice of his life. But this is not the end. On a later occasion, at the feast of the Dedication (10.22), there is a brief but electrifying debate between Jesus and the Jews. And here we find the real conclusion of the Shepherd allegory in verses 27–29. Naturally scholars have postulated accidental transposition to account for the apparent displacement. But this piece has been left over for its present position of set purpose. It is concerned with the eternal safety of the sheep. It follows on the point made earlier that the Shepherd lays down his life with the further purpose of taking it up again (verse 18). This means that he is in a position to give to the sheep eternal life. The prospect is assured, because it is not just Jesus' gift, but it is the will of the Father. So the sheep are safe, beyond the reach of hostile foes (verse 29). This is the end of the allegory, but it has paved the way for the shattering statement in verse 30: "I and the Father are one". But this statement does not belong to the allegory, though it derives its meaning from it. For of course the union expressed in this verse is first and foremost a moral union, as the subsequent verses show. The transition from the question in verse 24, "If you are the Christ, tell us plainly", to this daring and concise christological statement positively requires the tailpiece of the Shepherd allegory to define its meaning. Characteristically these verses both lead up to verse 30 and also delay it for greater emotional effect.

Our understanding of John's use of sources is now increasing, as we have seen how he uses sayings from the Jesus-tradition as the groundwork of the grand christological formulations of the discourses, and also how he uses items from the narrative-tradition to help to tie them into the sequence of the Gospel. We must now go a stage further, and see how he constructs a narrative quite apart from discourse. In point of fact John's method is very much the same as for the discourses. Similar techniques come into play. It is failure to recognize this which has led to a fatal lack of discrimination in the reconstruction of the hypothetical Signs Source.

Let us, then, take a look at the Witness of the Baptist and Call of the Disciples in 1.19–51. Both Becker and Fortna claimed virtually the whole of this long section for the Signs Source. They were untroubled by the fact that the author assumes that his readers will know about the baptism of Jesus, so that it can be referred to in a flashback (verse 32). Nor did they find anything odd about the total reorientation of "call" stories into "witness" stories. But if we think over this sequence in the light of the techniques already observed, I think it will become more likely that these unexpected features are due to radical recasting of the sources on John's part.

The sequence begins with a deputation to the Baptist to ask who he claims to be. This questioning could, of course, be derived from traditions about the Baptist not preserved elsewhere. But it is difficult to escape the impression that it is modelled on the questioning about *Jesus,* cf. Mark 6.14f; 8.27–9. Then follows a succession of short paragraphs or sequence of scenes, which is a style-feature identified as characteristic of John by J. Louis Martyn (op. cit., p. xxi). It is really the same as the sequences in the discourses, taking up the theme from various points of view. First, the Baptist is identified with the voice of prophecy, in a passage which has clear links with Synoptic material, even if it is consciously correcting earlier estimates of the Baptist (1.23–8). Next, the tradition of the baptism of Jesus is recast to lead up to the Baptist's testimony, using a messianic designation (the Son, or the Elect, of God, verse 34). Then the call of the disciples is described, with Andrew's assertion, "We have found the Messiah". We note in this paragraph the characteristic element of delay, or perhaps we should rather say in this case gradual recognition. Finally there is the incident of Nathanael, in which the conversation is carefully contrived to lead to the great testimony, "You are the Son of God! You are the King of Israel!"

The piece closes with a saying which summarizes the whole sequence, and makes it relevant to the experience of the reader as he addresses himself to the Gospel as a whole: "Amen, amen, I say to you, you will see heaven opened, and the angels of God ascending and descending upon the Son of man" (verse

51). The "Amen" opening once more suggests a basis in the Jesus-tradition (cf. Mark 14.62 and other Son of man sayings). It is correct to say that this verse hardly belongs to the preceding sequence, as the promoters of the Signs Source affirm. But it has been added by John when he used this quasi-homily for the continuous composition of the Gospel. He thereby relates the sequence, with its emphasis on the messiahship of Jesus, to the theology of the Gospel as a whole, in which the passion and the Son of man themes are so important.[9]

This account of the Baptist and the first disciples reads like a discourse in that it begins with a traditional element (the questioning, "Are you the Christ?", but addressed to the Baptist), and consists in a many-sided testimony ("He is the Christ", indicating Jesus). There is no logical progression, but the whole reaches an effective climax in the testimony of Nathanael. There are many typical Johannine touches. For example, in verse 37 the two disciples "follow" Jesus literally, and this anticipates their decision to "follow" him in discipleship. In verse 39 Jesus invites them to "see" where he is staying; this is the prelude to Andrew's confession of faith (verse 41), and ties up with the theme of sight which dominates the chapter.

But if so much is due to John's pen, we may well ask where are the items of historical tradition? Here we must recognize (against Fortna) that the creative composition places the precise underlying traditions beyond recovery. The section on the Baptist is the fruit of reflection on the tradition, but in fact John makes use of numerous words and phrases from the tradition, as can be seen from word-by-word comparison with the Synoptic parallels. The title "the lamb of God", however, can scarcely be part of this tradition. It is rather a fruit of reflection on the significance of Jesus' submission to John's baptism, and attests the apologetic need to explain this in the face of Jewish objections to Christian claims. The call of the first disciples has only a remote connection with the Synoptic tradition, but it does owe something to stereotyped call stories (cf. 21.19–22). The story of Nathanael, as Dodd points out, does not fall into a recognizable type of such stories, though it may be based on some such story as the Rich Young Ruler in Mark 10.17–22.

Here again apologetic motives are clearly at work, as the conversation turns on Nathanael's low estimate of Jesus' Galilean origins from a Jewish point of view. Nathanael himself is thus a representative figure, standing for the pious Jew whom the Christians still hope to be able to convert. The conclusion emerges that, whereas the earlier part of the sequence, dealing with the Baptist, has very clear links with underlying tradition, these links become progressively weaker, and the final item, on Nathanael, has only the barest connection with historical tradition. This is not unlike the way John's discourses move from a recognizable saying of Jesus to theological conclusions which go far beyond their starting-point.

Finally I would like to take a closer look at the Raising of Lazarus in the light of our observations of John's literary technique. This is another piece of extended narrative, and it is so difficult to chop up that Fortna retains nearly the whole of it for the Signs Source, in spite of the fact that it bristles with Johannisms all the way through. As far as the teaching goes, this story really provides nothing new which has not already been treated in the earlier discourses. That Jesus is "the resurrection and the life" (verse 25) has already been asserted in chapter 5. In any case the teaching of verses 24–26, splendid as it is, is not the climax of the composition, as it comes much too early. It is rather a necessary preliminary to give the reader the clue to understanding the story properly, not as the resuscitation of a dead man, but as a demonstration of the resurrection of Jesus himself. It is well known that the details of the story are carefully correlated with those of the resurrection narrative—the mourning women, the tomb closed with a stone, the grave-clothes and the face-cloth. In this way the reader is given a preview of the wonder which lies beyond the passion, to hold in his mind as he reads the solemn passion narrative, and so to guide his interpretation of it.

If, then, the story is not notable for introducing new teaching, but has this function of preparing the reader's mind for John's presentation of the passion of Jesus, we shall not be surprised to find that John's main concern is to produce a profound emotional impact. No exposition of this chapter is

adequate which fails to recognize that this is the overriding
consideration. Every reader must be conscious of this, for the
story reaches an unforgettable climax in the picture of Lazarus
emerging from the tomb. This never fails to impress, even if
we know the story so well that we lose altogether the sense of
surprise. But to read it for the first time is to experience something quite shattering. Nowhere is John's dramatic skill more
in evidence.

The story begins with the message of Mary and Martha that
Lazarus is ill. In the dialogue which follows there is a very
obvious and very characteristic play on the ideas of sleep and
death. But there is also a deeper undercurrent. For to respond
to the sisters' summons is to put Jesus' own life in danger of
death, as it means return to the danger-zone. It is underlined
by the dour remark of Thomas: "Let us also go, that we may
die with him". At this point, then, the thought of death is
uppermost, surrounded by a sense of anxiety and forboding.
Then it is discovered that Lazarus has already been dead four
days. This is an allusion to a Jewish legal technicality, that
death is not regarded as final and irreversible until after the
third day. There may be a hint here that Jesus' resurrection on
the third day was taken in some quarters as an admission that
he had never properly died. Whatever one thinks about that,
there can be no doubt about Lazarus. It was already the fourth
day. Whether this apologetic issue is intended or not, this detail
has in any case a necessary part to play in the subsequent
narrative (verse 39).

Once Jesus has arrived at Bethany, and discovered that
Lazarus has been dead so long, we are all prepared for him to
display his supernatural power (or rather manifest the glory of
God, cf. verse 4). But now John uses every possible device to
hold back the inevitable conclusion. First, there is the secret
conversation with Martha, which is important, because, as we
have seen, it gives the basis for a theological understanding of
what is to follow. Secondly, Mary comes to speak with Jesus.
The sisters could have come together, but it helps to retard the
narrative to make them come separately. Also Mary's function
is different from Martha's. There is no theological conversa-

tion. She heads a troop of mourners going to the tomb. The
emphasis falls on the element of grief. Jesus himself shares in
the grief (verse 33, where *enebrimesato* undoubtedly comes
from the source, though it may well have implied a different
emotion there).

John uses this feature with extraordinary skill, which the
casual reader may all too easily fail to observe. For he uses it
as the ostensible reason for the next step in the action. He
thereby hides the real purpose of Jesus' movements until the
last possible moment. Jesus asks to be taken to the tomb. It
can be assumed that this is a result of his grief, that he wants
to take a last look at the face of his dead friend. The fact that
no one is expecting him to raise Lazarus is emphasized by the
comment in verse 37: "Could not he who opened the eyes of
the blind man have kept this man from dying?" There is a
conscious irony here, for that is precisely what Jesus will do.
When they reach the tomb, there is further reference to Jesus'
emotion (with *embrimomenos* again from the source). He asks
for the stone to be removed. It is still supposed by everyone
present that this is in order to look on the dead man. Hence
Martha points out that it would be useless, as Lazarus is four
days dead. He would be unrecognizable. It is no accident that
it is Martha who points this out. By suddenly reintroducing
her into the narrative, John recaptures the little conversation
on the resurrection, and the reader is suddenly made aware of
what is going to happen.

But still the climax is postponed. Jesus stops to pray to the
Father. Light touches in the vocabulary show that this short
prayer is thematically related to the great prayer of Jesus before
the passion (ch. 17); it also has a certain relation to the prayer
of Jesus at Gethsemane in the Synoptic tradition. The prayer
as it stands here expresses the extreme urgency of the situation.
The miracle which is just about to be performed can all too
easily be misunderstood. It is essential that those who witness
it should perceive its true meaning as an act of God, testifying
to Jesus' derivation from the Father. Otherwise the whole purpose of it will be lost, and this final act of Jesus before his
passion will fail in its effect. And what applies to the miracle

itself applies also to the greater miracle which it anticipates. If the people fail to reach the true implications of the raising of Lazarus, how will they ever understand the passion and resurrection of Jesus himself?

It is against this highly charged background that John brings the narrative to a swift conclusion with the emergence of Lazarus from the tomb in response to Jesus' command. There is not the slightest interest in what happened to him afterwards, no hint of the family reunion or the immediate reaction of the bystanders. This is in complete contrast with the emphasis on the emotion of Jesus and of all those present in the preceding verses. But then that was to promote John's literary purpose, whereas now that the miracle has been performed it has made its impact, and nothing more needs to be said. It is far better to stop there, and let the whole thing sink into the mind of the reader.

The story which we have just reviewed is a most brilliant composition, a work of literary craftsmanship of the highest order. It is not to be expected that it might be carved up into a pre-Johannine story overlaid with Johannine touches.[10] The whole thing hangs together as a single piece. But that is not to say that it has no basis in the tradition. We have at any rate seen the use of *one* word from such a source! This seems but a paltry contribution to such a fine narrative, but it is important, as it certainly implies the use of a traditional story of some kind.

But before we can arrive at more precision about this, we must note that the *setting* of the story does not necessarily belong to it in the underlying tradition. The two sisters, Martha and Mary, are probably derived from the tradition which is used independently by Luke in 10.38–42. Their home is said to be at Bethany, because John has identified Mary with the woman who anointed Jesus there, whereas Luke had located their home in Galilee. Lazarus has been added to the family group in much the same way as John adds special characters into traditional settings in his handling of the resurrection traditions in chapter 20.[11] The name could be derived from the parable of Dives and Lazarus in Luke 16.19–31, which suggests his return from the grave. But in fact John shows no knowledge of this parable at all. The name either belonged to the raising story from the beginning, or became attached to it (perhaps by influence of the parable in its pre-Lucan form) before it reached John.

Whatever we think of this, we must assume that, in addition to the story of Martha and Mary which has provided the setting, John also had at his disposal a non-Synoptic story of the raising to life of a dead man. But apart from our one detail (*enebrimesato*) it is impossible to recover any of it at all. For there is a further element which in fact takes control of the telling of the actual incident, and that is the passion story of Jesus himself, so that the Gethsemane tradition lies behind the prayer, and the resurrection traditions provide the pictorial detail, and indeed the vocabulary to a considerable degree. The only clue to the underlying story is the fact that John's use of *enebrimesato* is unusual. Properly it expresses anger rather than grief. John has only secured for it this meaning by introducing a parallel phrase from his normal vocabulary. In the original story it may perhaps have expressed the energy required for performing the miracle, as Campbell Bonner has suggested in his study of this word in the light of pagan parallels.[12] If so, the feature of calling the man out of the grave is possibly original too. But the similarity of this idea to Jewish legendary notions about resurrection forbid certainty on this point (cf. Matt. 27.52f, and John's own more sophisticated counterpart of it in 5.28f). There really is nothing of the underlying story left apart from this one word. We can only say that John did use a raising story, comparable to the traditions of Jairus' daughter and the son of the widow of Nain. But his treatment of it, as a grand set piece before the passion narrative, has covered it up completely.

In this chapter we have looked at a number of John's compositions—the discourses, the use of traditional miracle stories in conjunction with discourse, and the treatment of extended narrative. The traditional material includes both story-items and sayings from the Jesus-tradition. Many of the compositions are sufficiently self-contained to suggest that they existed independently in the first instance as homilies addressed to John's Church, in a situation where there is close contact with Judaism and a lively debate between Church and Synagogue. The peculiar feature of holding over part of a homily for use in the next section of the continuous narrative gives some idea of the process by which the Gospel came to be written. It can be seen as a response to the request of his audience that he should put his homilies into some permanent form. And the literary form which John chooses is that of the Gospel, already achieved by Mark. The Gospel has a plan and a plot of its own, and is not merely a matter of stitching together the existing homilies. We must assume that much of it is new matter, composed specifically for the Gospel as it now stands. On the other hand, certain sections stand so much apart from the main course of the narrative, that it is reasonable to suppose that John has done the work in more than one stage. He has revised and considerably expanded his work for a second edition. I hold that chapter 6, on the Bread of Life, and 11.1–44, the story of Lazarus which we have just examined, belong to the second edition. This has to some extent obscured the original plan of the Gospel, which is more coherent when they are dropped. Our study of the Fourth Gospel will not be complete if we do not look at this synthetic work of the making of the Gospel, and see how John has built his theology on the traditions which he uses. This will be the subject of the final chapter.

4 THE THEOLOGY OF THE FOURTH GOSPEL

The main task which we set before us in this book was to uncover the sources of the Fourth Gospel. We have seen that there is a good case to assume that John's work is the product of an elaborate process of composition. Indeed the problems of the text as it stands are too great to admit of a simple solution. The attempt to show that it is a redaction of continuous sources must also be regarded as unsuccessful for this reason. The so-called Signs Source is not a single document which can be isolated from the rest without remainder. It is rather an assembly of units of tradition which came to John in the form of short collections or independent pieces, which he has used selectively and often adapted drastically. The traditions available to John also included sayings of Jesus, parables, and proverbs, which have a fundamental position in the composition of the discourses. The discourses are not a Christian rewriting of a series of poems about the gnostic myth of the Revealer, but are compositions of the evangelist himself on the basis of the sayings at his disposal. Although these compositions are best thought of as homilies delivered to the Christian assembly, they embody issues of vital importance in the Christian and Jewish debate in the time when John was writing. They therefore sometimes have the form of a rabbinic disputation. This is indeed particularly clear in the case of the discourse on the Bread of Life in chapter 6, which turns on the exegesis of the manna tradition of Exod. 16. But in every case the impression remains of a homily, of the *preaching* of the gospel, because of the way in which John handles his material. He uses what can only be described as rhetorical skill to build up to a climax which makes a compelling emotional impact. And if this is true of the longer units of composition, it is surely true too of the structure of the Gospel as a whole. In order to appreciate this, we shall have to take some broad sweeps through the Gospel, and many issues will have to be left on one side, or only very lightly touched. But we shall be able to make use of what has already been observed in the passages reviewed in the last chapter.

The Gospel as a whole falls neatly into two parts, the ministry of Jesus and the passion narrative. It will not be necessary for us to consider the second of these in detail. For its climactic effect and emotional power in relation to the rest of the Gospel need no demonstration. As for the rest, it is customary to make the division at the end of chapter 12. The opening verses of chapter 13 (the Last Supper) have an extreme solemnity which makes them an introduction to the passion as a whole. Thus Becker takes part of chapter 12 as belonging to the Signs Source. But Fortna is more realistic when he connects chapter 12 with the passion narrative, for the contents of it certainly belong to the fixed form of the passion narrative, as we can see from the Synoptic parallels. So it seems that we must make the literary division at the end of chapter 11 instead. But I have suggested that the Raising of Lazarus was an addition by John for the second edition of his Gospel. The remainder of the chapter, on the Priests' Plot, certainly belongs with chapter 12. This takes us back to the end of chapter 10 for the close of the first part of the Gospel in its original form. It is here that we shall find the climax to which all the rest has been leading.

When we look at the beginning, to find our point of departure, we again have to take into account additions for the second edition. There is a notable aporia in the Prologue, where verses about John the Baptist interrupt the measured flow of the composition. There is much to be said for the view that the Prologue was written later than the main narrative of the Gospel, which began originally with 1.6–7a and continued with 1.19. The first division of the Gospel can, then, be defined as 1.19 through to the end of chapter 10. But not all of the material within these limits belongs to the first edition. The Cleansing of the Temple in 2.13–22 has probably been transferred to this position from chapter 12, where it originally belonged as part of the passion narrative. John put it into its present position as a result of the dislocation caused by his decision to insert the

Raising of Lazarus.[1] There has perhaps been some dislocation in chapter 3, but in spite of the difficulties I am disposed to regard it as preserving the original form. But the great discourse of chapter 6 clearly interrupts the sequence. Rather than transposing it to a different position, for example, before chapter 5, I feel it is best to regard this as another fresh addition for the second edition of the work. It must therefore be disregarded in our survey of the first division of the Gospel in its original form. In any case the *pericope de adultera* (7.53—8.11) is to be excluded as a non-Johannine addition, which only crept into the text in the second or third century.

So the first division begins with the Testimony of the Baptist and ends at 10.42. Looking at the end, we see, perhaps with some surprise, a final allusion to the position of the Baptist (10.41). E. Bammel has argued that this is a fragment from the Signs Source,[2] but it seems to me to be much more in line with John's own editorial style. It is, then, a case of "inclusio", whereby the final comment recalls the opening sequence, and so encapsulates all that comes in between. This is a well-known homiletic device. In the beginning the Baptist had testified that Jesus is the Son (or Elect) of God (1.34), and this testimony had been filled out with the other titles in the rest of chapter 1, ending with the picture of the anticipated glory of the Son of man in 1.51. Now, at the end of chapter 10, this testimony can be referred to as something that has been demonstrated in the course of the ministry of Jesus which comes in between. This will lead us to expect that this is precisely the purpose of John's presentation of Jesus in the intervening chapters. The whole of the ministry is a demonstration of the meaning of Jesus for faith. Each episode, and each discourse and debate with the Jews, is aimed at fulfilling this purpose.

We need not go back over the opening sequence, 1.19–51. It is narrative in discourse style, which presents the titles of Jesus. The Marriage at Cana in 2.1–12 simply rounds this off with a tale that symbolizes the arrival of something new in the history of salvation, the new wine of the messianic age replacing the old. Then in chapter 3 John begins to unfold his theme.

Obviously we cannot go into this chapter in detail. But we can at least make a correct general assessment of its place in John's scheme, if we take notice once more of its basis in the tradition of the sayings of Jesus. This, as we should expect, is indicated by the "Amen" opening of Jesus' reply to Nicodemus: "Unless one is born anew, he cannot see the kingdom of God". It is a version of the saying preserved in Matt. 18.3: "Amen, I say to you, unless you turn and become like children, you will never enter the kingdom of heaven". The whole piece is concerned with the radical reorientation of the mind which is required of those who are brought face to face with Jesus. In the course of the following verses the issue is sharpened to bring home the crisis of decision which this involves. It is here that the language becomes most reminiscent of hellenistic dualism, and we may well wonder whether John has derived his thought from gnostic sources. John asserts that the radical reorientation of the mind is necessary because of the unique position of Jesus himself. Consequently the thought fastens on the contrast between the heavenly origin of Jesus and the earthly origin of all other sources of knowledge. This is worked out in moral terms in 3.16–21, where John is clearly indebted to the Qumran type of distinction between the two spirits in men, the angel of light and the angel of darkness. In the final paragraph, 3.31–6, it is tempting to see a more radical dualism between the heavenly and the earthly, but this is really a mistake. The point here is the same as was made at the beginning of the discourse, that spiritual things must be spiritually discerned, and Jesus conveys the whole truth of God unstintingly to those who will believe. But the fact remains that Jesus appears in these verses as the Revealer of God, and it is this which raises the thorny problem of hellenistic influence. We shall be wise to reserve judgement on this issue until we have traced the whole process of thought in the first ten chapters.

So now we pass on to chapter 4, the Conversation with the Woman of Samaria at Jacob's Well. Here Jesus is presented as the giver of the living water. At once we are faced with the same problem of hellenistic influence. But let us still be cautious, for water symbolism is far too frequent in the Old Testament and Judaism to be a necessary pointer in this direction. The crucial thing is what John does with this symbolism. And here we have his comment in the shape of a complete break in the conversation at verse 16. The issue of the woman's five husbands (which in my opinion has nothing whatever to do with the five pagan nations with which Samaria was populated according to 2 Kings 17.24) has changed the subject to Jesus' prophetic insight. The whole thing leads up to its climax in the statement that he is the Messiah (4.25f). But as this is set in terms of Samaritan ideas, it really conveys much more the notion that he is the expected Prophet. From this point of view Jesus can be regarded as the Revealer of truth, the conveyor of the living water, within the frame of Jewish and Samaritan ideas about prophecy. The section concludes with a miracle from traditional sources, the story of the Official's Son at Capernaum (4.46–54). This is not reproduced straight, but has been specially adapted to provide a practical demonstration of the gift of life which Jesus has claimed to be able to give.

Looking back over both chapters 3 and 4, we can see that they are treating the same theme, but from opposite angles. Chapter 3 was concerned with the spiritual capacity to *receive* the eternal life which Jesus has come to give. Chapter 4 is concerned with the *nature* of this eternal life which the spiritual person may expect to receive. Whether as the one to whom men respond, or as the one who gives life to men, Jesus is depicted as the channel of the whole of God's good will for mankind. We are no further on as far as the question of hellenistic influence is concerned. What we have seen is John's reinterpretation of the meaning of the kingdom of God, the central item of Jesus' preaching according to the primitive tradition. It is the state which John calls eternal life, which results from response to Jesus. John's interpretation shares with the primitive tradition the essential aspect of personal challenge.

With chapter 5 the Gospel enters a fresh phase. Now we have the series of open disputes between Jesus and the Jews at Jerusalem. These are taken up with the question of Jesus' credentials. The claims about him have already been stated in chapters 3 and 4. Now it must be shown that these are no vain boasts but the sober truth. The central factor which can be drawn from the preceding two chapters is that Jesus is the giver of life. But that is to arrogate a function which belongs to God alone. Hence the argument of these controversial chapters is mainly directed to establishing the truth about the relationship between Jesus and God. Here, then, we may hope to gain some greater precision about the origins of John's thought.

The cardinal point of chapter 5 has already been explained in the last chapter. It is the fact that Jesus *does* perform the functions of God, by delegation from God and at his express command. "I can do nothing on my own authority" (5.30). We saw how this teaching was based on the parable of the Apprenticed Son (5.19). Here we observe that the definition of these divine functions is correlated with conventional Jewish expectations about the Son of man. The fact that John can use this theme in joint harness with the rest of the material is not due to later retouching by a Jewish-Christian editor, but to the fact that the whole debate is conducted on Jewish ground. The idea of this eschatological figure is common ground between John and his Jewish opponents, and is also an irreducible feature of the authentic Jesus-tradition. But that does not mean that John fails to use it creatively. In fact his personal contribution is to be found in the assertion that Jesus does now, in his earthly ministry, acts which anticipate his functions as Son of man at the End of the Age. And this brings to the surface the threefold correlation which really explains John's whole presentation of Jesus in the first ten chapters, which we are passing in rapid review:

(a) The signs, such as the healing of the paralytic with which chapter 5 opens, *demonstrate* Jesus' future work as Son of man, and so in different ways show him giving life.

(b) The invitation of Jesus to men to respond to him in faith *anticipates* the coming judgement (e.g. 5.25, "the hour is coming, *and now is* . . .").

(c) But the ultimate fulfilment in the future is not denied. John retains the consistent eschatology of his Jewish background. His eschatology is neither "realized" nor timeless.

We now have to skip chapter 6, and come to the highly complex literary assemblage of chapters 7 and 8. I will deal with them only very briefly. The one point I want to emphasize here is that, once more, the terms of the debate are set out entirely in Jewish categories. Some of the material in chapter 7 is concerned with the issue of messiahship. Does Jesus fulfil the conditions required for a messianic claimant? This is clearly a matter of the Jewish and Christian debate. The only point where the possibility of hellenistic concepts emerges is the little paragraph about the water in 7.37–9. The odd thing about this little piece is that it is not developed into a discourse. I hold that it was part of one of John's homilies, which he decided not to use in full, as it would have overlapped the similar discourse on the Water of Life in chapter 4. Bultmann, correctly in my view, regards 7.37 as a Wisdom invitation with an eschatological reference. Those who refuse to drink will pay for it at the coming judgement. It thus introduces the theme of division between believing and unbelieving Jews.

The same really applies also to the saying "I am the light of the world" in 8.12. The theme of light is not developed from the point of view of the revelation of knowledge. It is again concerned with judgement, the light which reveals true from false. This again is a specially Jewish emphasis, found also in the Dead Sea Scrolls (for further details of this passage, cf. the first chapter). In spite of this, however, the context contains the most uncompromisingly dualistic language in the whole of the Gospel: "You are from below, I am from above; you are of this world, I am not of this world" (8.23). But again it is necessary to be very wary before jumping to the conclusion that John is committed to a fundamental dualism. It is really much more like the flesh and spirit dualism of chapter 3, though expressed in spatial terms. Jesus speaks the truth of God, because he is derived from God. The Jews prefer falsehood, because they have sided with the world apart from God. This does not mean that the world is inherently evil. For in the discourse which follows in the later part of chapter 8 (which was our point of departure in the previous chapter), the distinction between Jesus and the Jews is put into yet another set of correla-

tives: Jesus is the Son of the Father, whereas they are the sons
of the devil (8.44). The dualism goes no further than that of the
Qumran doctrine of the two spirits in man.

If we now try to put this complicated central section into the
larger frame of chapters 1–10, we can see that it marks an ad-
vance on the position which had been reached in chapter 5.
There Jesus had defended his claim to perform functions which
properly belong to God alone, on the grounds that he is the Son
of man to whom God will in any case delegate these functions.
Now the thought is not so much concerned with Jesus' future
functions as with his origins, the relationship which he bears to
God, which fits him for this unique position. The argument
proceeds by contrasts, so that the deeper one delves into the
mystery of Jesus, the more clearly one sees how deep-seated is
the opposition to him. The thought of the passion is never far
away. The argument begins with human origins, whether Jesus'
birthplace was correct for a messianic claimant, etc. It passes
on to spiritual origins. He is the Son of the Father, whereas the
Jews are sons of the devil. Finally, it moves magnificently to
the further consequence that Jesus comes, as it were, out of the
timelessness of God. He is the expression of the Wisdom of
God, which was in the beginning with God. This way of speaking of Jesus' pre-existence by means of the Jewish Wisdom
tradition is not new in John. It already has ample precedents in
the letters of Paul.[3] Its importance for John will become clearer
when we turn to the additional pieces which John included in
his second edition.

The argument of the first division of the Gospel comes to
its conclusion in another complex compilation, chapters 9 and
10. Chapter 9 is narrative in discourse style, based on a Synoptic-type miracle of the healing of a man born blind. It follows up the theme of light as the capacity for discernment, and
so the man's restored sight (or rather newly created sight) is his
capacity for faith. At the conclusion of the chapter the Pharisees turn out to be those who are blind. Thus the stage is set
for the final revelation about Jesus, which men will either accept by faith or reject through blindness. Thus the issue of
Christology is the cause of the final rejection of Jesus, and the

passion is the inevitable consequence. Before, however, this decisive moment is reached, John inserts the allegory of the Shepherd in 10.1–18. The sudden change of literary genre seems at first surprising. But it is perfectly consistent with John's methods. It is in a sense an example of his use of delaying tactics, as he holds off the climax, to make it more impressive when it is actually reached. But it also serves a positive function, by laying out the categories of thought for the climax itself. The allegory (verses 7–18), based on the two parables in verses 1–5, is constructed in typical discourse style, one facet after another being picked up and developed, until the conclusion is reached that Jesus gives up his life voluntarily in response to the Father's will for the eternal salvation of the sheep.

Then at the Feast of Dedication, on an entirely fresh occasion, the crunch comes. The Jews ask Jesus outright whether he claims to be the Messiah. It is the answer to this question which constitutes the final revelation of the truth about Jesus. By way of leading into this crucial statement, John uses, as we have seen, a further element of the Shepherd allegory which he has left over, to my mind purposely left over, for this dramatic moment. It is the assurance that the sheep, i.e. those who respond in faith to Jesus, can never be snatched from him, because they are the Father's own gift to Jesus. The Jews may do their worst, but because even Jesus' death at their hands is a voluntary sacrifice on his part, done in obedience to the Father, they cannot succeed in disposing of him. This is the thought which prepares for the final statement: "I and the Father are one" (10.30). The statement is so bold and uncompromising that it provokes the ultimate reaction. The Jews condemn Jesus for blasphemy, "because you, being a man, make yourself God" (10.33). But the believer—and, John hopes, the discerning reader of his splendid composition—knows that it is the simple truth. Jesus, as the designated Son of man who performs the divine functions of judging and giving life, and as the Wisdom of God which was in the beginning with God, is in perfect moral union with the Father. To put faith in Jesus is to entrust oneself in him to God. It is not without significance that the whole context emphasizes the moral aspect of Jesus' union with God, rather than the metaphysical.

Now it is highly important to observe the basis which this grand finale has in the underlying tradition. Like the episode of the Man Born Blind, and like the allegory of the Shepherd, here too John is building on the traditions which were central to the early Church's memories of Jesus and an essential part of the Synoptic record. For the question in verse 24, "If you are the Christ, tell us plainly", belongs to the tradition of the trial of Jesus before the high priest. Jesus' prevaricating answer has a parallel in Luke 22.67. The accusation of blasphemy is precisely the charge in the Synoptic trial. But John formulates it differently. Whereas according to the synoptists Jesus claims to share God's throne as Son of man, here we have the same notion in the most concise form possible, "I and the Father are one". The blasphemy is the same, for in both cases Jesus puts himself on an equality with God. It is in my opinion a mistake to suppose that John means by this concise phrase actual identity between Jesus and God. Still Jewish concepts apply, rather than hellenistic. I hold that John has consciously and deliberately made use of the trial tradition for the climax of his great christological exposition, occupying the whole of the first division of the Gospel. The omission of the real substance of the trial before the high priest in chapter 18 is thus no accident. It is missing, because John has used it already. This observation, incidentally, shows how careful one has to be in comparing John's passion narrative with the Synoptic accounts. His omissions are not necessarily due to the lack of anything similar in his source.

In the original form of the Gospel the story of Jesus' ministry ended with the little note in 10.41, recalling the testimony of the Baptist with which it began. Then followed chapter 12, including the Cleansing of the Temple (now in chapter 2) and the Priests' Plot (now in chapter 11) *after* the Triumphal Entry. So the passion narrative begins. But we have already decided not to go through that, for the moment, as it would deflect us from our present purpose. What we have still to do is, first, to make a general comment on the relation of the christological exposition of the first ten chapters of the Gospel to the earlier tradition, and secondly, to assess the purpose of the major additions which John inserted in the second edition of his work.

For our first point we must use exactly the same method as we used for the examination of individual units in the last chapter. John's methods as a writer must be assessed before we draw conclusions about his use of old traditions. Looking back over the first ten chapters, we can see that, in spite of the jumble of literary units which they contain, the whole sequence really has much the same pattern as a discourse. The first section in 1.19–51, itself a narrative in discourse style, sets the theme for the whole. The christological titles there displayed announce the fact that the Gospel is to be an essay in Christology. Just as in the individual discourses, the exposition of this basic text does not follow a logical progression, but picks up one facet of Christology after another. The relationship of the successive chapters to the first one is admittedly very loose, but it is at least permissible to see a link between the testimony of the Baptist in 1.19–34 and chapters 3 and 4, because of the baptismal themes which they contain; between the eschatological character of the latter part of those verses and the theme of the Functions of the Son of man in chapter 5; between the messianic designation in the Call of the Disciples in 1.35–42 and the messianic debate in chapter 7; and between the theme of the origins of Jesus in the story of Nathanael in 1.43–50 and in the discourse of chapter 8. Finally, the saying about the Son of man in 1.51 is probably a variant of the very saying in the trial of Jesus before the high priest which is the Synoptic counterpart to the blasphemy of chapter 10 (cf. Mark 14.62). Seeing that John is using material which he originally composed for the most part as independent pieces, we cannot expect the relationship to be very close. But, even if the sequence has no very logical progression, it is not simply episodic. It is so ordered that it moves steadily towards its climax. This is the more impressive in its emotional impact, because the progress towards the climax of thought runs *pari passu* with the mounting tension of the hardening opposition to Jesus. By the time the end is reached the reader cannot escape seeing the personal decision of faith as quite literally a matter of life and death.

If we may judge by the parallel of the individual discourses, we should naturally expect the underlying tradition to be contained in the opening section, the rest being an exposition of it. From this point of view the christological titles in chapter 1 are not only the text on which the rest is built, but also comprise the traditional christological foundation. It is true that John does not expound them title by title, but we have seen that there is a certain relationship between them and the themes of the central chapters. What is more to the point is that this observation of method puts into its place the widely canvassed idea that the "I am" sayings are the foundation of John's Christology. In fact they are rather the *consequences* of his Christology. It is because John *arrives at* a Wisdom Christology in his attempt to expound Jesus' origins, that he uses this formula from time to time to express the gift of Jesus in terms of a Wisdom invitation. But we should note that only *one* such saying actually occurs in the first edition of the Gospel (8.12; the sayings in 10.7, 9, 11, 14 only identify Jesus with items in the parable, and so are not relevant).[4] When we come to further detail, we know already from our previous study that traditional sayings lie at the heart of the individual discourses. Thus he expounds the titles with the aid of sayings from the Jesus-tradition. His ideas are in line with earlier sayings, even if they take them further than their original meaning. Thus the close relationship of the Father and the Son is a feature of some Synoptic sayings. We can think of the Q passage, Matt. 11.27: "All things have been delivered to me by my Father, etc." The idea that Jesus is one sent by the Father appears in Matt. 10.40, "He who receives me receives him who sent me", and many similar passages.

Even if some verses, and some of the ideas with which John develops his thought on this foundation, owe a debt to hellenistic thought, the terms of the argument are in wholly Jewish categories. The issues of messiahship and of the Son of man figure are read off from Jewish eschatological and apocalyptic speculation. The dualism never really goes beyond the form of

dualism known to be current in the Judaism of the time. The
function of Jesus as the Revealer has less in common with the
hellenistic myth of the *theios anēr* than with the Jewish Wisdom tradition in its later use as a means of expressing the uni-
versal and ultimate revelation of God in the Law. But we may
grant a little interaction of ideas in the cosmopolitan milieu of
John's world. To those who do think in hellenistic terms there
is certainly a danger here. John can all too easily be taken to
mean that Jesus is not really a human being, but a god in
human dress. Käsemann indeed argues that this is really what
John does mean, and that, so far from opposing docetism
(which is what Hoskyns took to be the main purpose of the
Gospel), he is himself a docetist. The difficulty is that John
does not set out his position systematically. The relationship
of Jesus to the Father appears to have cosmic implications, but
these are never precisely explained. There can be little doubt
that John's readers were not sure what he meant. It is not
irrelevant to note that it was among gnostic Christians that
John was first appreciated. Some at least of John's additions to
the Gospel for the second edition seem to me to be intended to
clarify this problem.

So we come to our second point, the purpose of the major
additions. First there is the Prologue, 1.1–18. If it is correct
to regard this as a piece welded into the original opening about
the Baptist, it must have been composed as an independent
unit to begin with. This fact, coupled with the elevated and
measured style of the composition, has led numerous scholars
to suppose that it is based on a Semitic Wisdom poem. Numerous reconstructions have been attempted, the most recent being
that of J. C. O'Neill.[5] None is really convincing. But our
observations on John's technique in the first edition will naturally lead us to a different solution. It is yet another example of
John's discourse style, composed like so many of the discourses
as a separate piece before incorporation into the Gospel. The
opening statement in verses 1–5 is worked over afresh in successive phases of interpretation, first to show how the light that
is never quenched enters the souls of men through faith (verses
10–13), and then to show how this source of life became flesh

and revealed God in a way that surpasses the revelation to Moses on Sinai (verses 14, 16–18). The final verse characteristically recalls the opening phrase ("the only God") and constitutes a most impressive climax ("made him known" puts the idea of the Logos into the form of a verb). This way of understanding the Prologue has received confirmation from a recent article by P. Borgen,[6] who compares John's method with the method of exposition of scripture in the Jerusalem Targum.

The purpose of the Prologue is precisely to answer the demand which we have already felt for a more systematic exposition of the cosmic implications of John's Christology. I think John composed it because the first edition revealed this need. And again we observe how Jewish rather than hellenistic categories predominate. John uses "Logos" instead of "Wisdom", but his composition is certainly modelled on the Wisdom poems of Prov. 8.22ff and Sir. 24. The targumic method noted by Borgen also marks it out as Jewish. Moreover, it incorporates a vital issue of the debate between Church and Synagogue, the relation between the revelation of God in Jesus and the supposedly definitive revelation in the Law. Again, the idea of the Logos becoming flesh is not the climax of the piece, as is so often assumed (for the climax is in verse 18), but it does nevertheless preclude the docetic interpretation to which John's expressions elsewhere may give rise. Finally, the Prologue has numerous links of word and phrase and theme with the christological teaching of the first ten chapters, especially with the discourse with Nicodemus in chapter 3. John writes the Prologue in full view of what he has already written, to provide the rational framework of his teaching.

The second major addition is the discourse on the Bread of Life in chapter 6. Some attention has already been given to this in the last chapter. The discourse follows John's usual style. It is based on the manna text of Exod. 16. Now we must observe the significance of the other quotation in verse 45: "And they shall all be taught by God" (Isa. 54.13). *Taught*: that is the point. The manna tradition, the feeding of God's people, is interpreted in terms of the provision of the true teaching. Borgen[7] and others[8] have shown that John is here drawing on a

Jewish midrashic tradition, in which the miracle of the manna was taken as a type of the gift of the Law of Moses. John's point is that Jesus himself, in his flesh which was crucified, is the true teaching, the true heavenly food. Thus this magnificent discourse fastens on the same issues as the Prologue, the relation of the revelation in Jesus to the Law, and the reality of his flesh and passion, which combats docetism. The reason why John has inserted this chapter between chapters 5 and 7 now becomes apparent. It is because the discourse is a splendid example of scriptural exegesis. It illustrates how Moses "wrote" concerning Jesus, the very thing which Jesus has just claimed in 5.46. The chapter is thus precisely in its proper position, even if it is an afterthought, and theories of transposition really miss the point.

The introduction of the Raising of Lazarus into the second edition, with its far-reaching effects on the ordering of the opening sequence of the passion narrative, need not be reviewed again. But I must say a word about the additions to the passion narrative itself, which John has inserted in the second edition, because these bring in other issues arising after he had finished the first edition of the Gospel.

In its original form the passion narrative followed fairly closely the established pattern which we find in the Synoptic Gospels. The Priests' Plot (11.47–53) followed the Triumphal Entry (12.12–19) and the Cleansing of the Temple (now in 2.13–22). It is possible that the Anointing at Bethany (12.1–8) originally came after this, at the end of the chapter, and that it has been transferred to an earlier position to bring it into closer relation with the Lazarus story. The teaching which follows these events in the Synoptic tradition does not belong to John's scheme, though he has at this point his own composition, which incorporates elements of the Gethsemane tradition (12.20–36a). Thereafter John's first edition had his account of the Last Supper and the first Supper Discourse (chapters 13 and 14). And the point to notice about this is that, though the Last Supper account is based on traditional material, it has been reshaped with the sole purpose of teaching the lessons of discipleship.[9] This theme is expanded further in the discourse of chapter 14. Next came the departure of Jesus and the disciples (14.31: "Rise, let us go hence") to Gethsemane (18.1).

The rest of John's passion narrative does not seem to have undergone any changes for the second edition. We may note here briefly its relation to the underlying tradition. The Gethsemane account is confined to the arrest of Jesus (18.2–11), because the tradition of the agony has already been used in chapter 12, though an echo of it remains in 18.11. The trial before the high priest (18.12–27)[10] is similarly defective, because John has used the central item of it in chapter 10, as we have seen. It is thus largely confined to the related tradition of Peter's denials. The trial before Pilate (18.28—19.16), on the other hand, is based on the same feature as the Synoptic parallels, i.e. the issue of kingship. John has handled this tradition very freely in order to extract from it every ounce of irony and to build up to a dramatic climax. The sequence shows all his skill as a literary craftsman. Moreover, John's treatment of the traditional theme is comparable to his work in the discourses. Finally the crucifixion (19.17–30), burial (19.31–42), and resurrection (20) accounts consist of a similarly free and creative treatment of traditional items, this time using the technique of a sequence of scenes, as in chapter 1. They are aimed at gently reducing the emotional tension, so as to leave the reader with an impression of confidence and faith. The theme of discipleship, enunciated in chapters 13 and 14, comes back suitably into prominence in the resurrection scenes of chapter 20.

The additions for the second edition are concerned with reinforcing the theme of discipleship in the light of the greatly increased danger to the Church since the first edition was written. These new pieces consist of the second Supper Discourse in chapters 15 and 16, which is a patchwork of John's homiletic material, including the allegory of the Vine, and also the Prayer of Jesus in chapter 17. Both of these are concerned with the future of the Church in the post-resurrection situation. Both exhibit the deepest concern for the fidelity of the disciples in the coming time of testing. In view of the Jewish awareness elsewhere in the Gospel, we shall probably be wise to see here the threat of Jewish persecution of Christians, rather than that of the Roman imperial power, though this may also be a factor. This new emphasis may well reflect a change for the worse in Jewish and Christian relationships, especially if the edict excluding Christians from the synagogue was promulgated in the interval between the first and second editions of John's work. I cannot accept Käsemann's contention that the Jewish character of the debates is a sort of local colour, and that they are a cover for a deeper debate between John's Christology and the religion of the wider hellenistic world.

But certainly in these pieces the thought extends to the mission of the disciples to the world at large. The disciples are to pass on the revelation which has actually been displayed in the life of Jesus, his acts and his passion. And this revelation in the last analysis is contained in the statement, "I and the Father are one". When speaking of this earlier, I described this as primarily a moral union. It is this profoundly ethical outlook which reappears in the way John expresses the very same point in the final words of the Prayer of Jesus: "That the love with which thou hast loved me may be in them, and I in them". It is difficult to believe that, in a statement such as this, John is dependent on an extraneous religious tradition, however much the language of love may be a commonplace of the higher religion of Hellenism. The prayer of chapter 17 has a strength of emotion, an intensity, and a sense of urgency, in spite of its fundamental calm assurance that Jesus has himself already won the spiritual victory even before the passion is begun. The most natural explanation of this is that John is here giving vent to his own passionate concern for the Church; and the language of the loving union of the Father and the Son, which is accessible to the disciples who believe in Jesus, is nothing else than the deepest expression of John's own personal spiritual experience as a Christian.

Behind the Fourth Gospel there lies the intense evangelistic concern of one who is deeply committed to the finality of the revelation of God in the Jesus of history for faith. The identity of the evangelist is lost in the mists of time. But his mind, his creative skill, and indeed his heart and soul, are plain for all to see in the work which has come from his hands. John draws his

material from the traditions of Jesus' words and acts which
were already circulating, and from the story of the passion,
which had already reached fixed form in the liturgy of the
Christian Passover. His work begins by being a series of homilies, as disjointed and unconnected as the sources which he
had at his disposal. But the Gospel form had already been
produced by at least one of his older contemporaries, John
Mark. John's presentation of his material in this form is no
mere copying of Mark, but is dominated by the circumstances
of his own place and time. He is at the centre of debate between
Christians and Jews, at a point where the breach between
Church and Synagogue is already irrevocable, if not quite abso-
lute. With the passage of time the centre of interest has shifted
from the Kingdom preached by Jesus to the person of Jesus
himself, and so to the meaning of Jesus. The debate is no
longer conducted at the level of Jesus' credentials for messiahship (though these are recalled in chapter 7), but at the level of
his relationship with God. The Jews sent Jesus to Pilate on the
charge of claiming to be the King-Messiah (18.33). But this
charge can just as well be put in the form "He has made himself the Son of God" (19.7). To say "I am the Son of God" is
exactly equivalent to saying "I and the Father are one" (10.30,
33, 36). If we feel a lack of precision here, and wish to object
that such expressions are not exact equivalents; and if we feel
that John's use of the Wisdom ideas fails to draw a clear line
between ethical and metaphysical concepts; we are entitled to
see in this very confusion a strong indication that John's
thought does not operate in a Greek philosophical mould.

In so far as it is permissible to look for polemical aims in the
Fourth Gospel, it is Jewish objections to Christianity which are
the chief concern, and constitute the most powerful formative
influence over John's thought. But influence is not the same
thing as purpose. The purpose of the Fourth Gospel is to bring
men to faith. It is summed up in the well-known words of
20.31: "That you may believe that Jesus is the Christ, the Son
of God, and that believing you may have life in his name". But
these words are not to be interpreted according to the pale ghost
of John's theology in the hypothetical (I think chimerical

Signs Source, of which they never were the conclusion; nor even in the light of an attempt to correct the inadequacy of this source, as Bultmann suggests; but rather in the light of the Christology of the Gospel as a whole, which embodies John's own deepest Christain faith.

NOTES

CHAPTER 1

1. Cf. C. K. Barrett, *The New Testament Background: Selected Documents* (S.P.C.K. 1956), p. 167.
2. For the debate on this issue see E. Earle Ellis, *The Gospel of Luke* (*The Century Bible, New Edition*) (Nelson 1966), pp. 55-8.
3. "Source Criticism and Religionsgeschichte in the Fourth Gospel", in *Jesus and Man's Hope* (Pittsburgh Theological Seminary 1970), vol. I, pp. 247-73.
4. For a very recent analysis of the Prologue see Peder Borgen, "Observations on the Targumic Character of the Prologue of John", *New Testament Studies* 16 (April 1970), pp. 288-95. While I am in general sympathy with the author's position, I do not think he has made out his case for regarding verses 6-8 as an original part of the plan of the Prologue.
5. Detailed evidence in justification of the statements made here will be found in my forthcoming commentary.

CHAPTER 2

1. A popular introduction to redaction criticism is provided by N. Perrin, *What is Redaction Criticism?* (S.P.C.K. 1970).
2. *NTS* 16 (January 1970), pp. 130-48.
3. SNTS Monograph Series 11 (C.U.P. 1970).
4. Cf. Bornkamm, Barth, and Held, *Tradition and Interpretation in Matthew* (1963).
5. Cf. E. Käsemann, *The Testament of Jesus* (The New Testament Library) (S.C.M. Press 1968), p. 26.

CHAPTER 3

1. In verse 31 omit *pepisteukotas autō* ("who had believed in him") with C. H. Dodd, R. E. Brown. The words are probably a harmonizing addition, assuming a close connection between verses 30 and 31b. But though they are found in all manuscripts they cannot be right, as the subsequent dialogue shows.

2. At the end of the verse omit *tēs hamartias* ("to sin") with D b sy⁵ Clem. What the verse means is that the slave (in the parable which is just about to follow) is everyone who commits sin.

3. To this extent J. C. H. Lebram is correct in asserting with regard to chapter 6 that the discourse has the *Stilform* of a *schriftgelehrte Diskussion*, and is not a true rabbinic homily; cf. his review of B. J. Malina, *The Palestinian Manna Tradition*, in *Vetus Testamentum* xx (1970), pp. 124-8.

4. As argued by J. Louis Martyn, *History and Theology in the Fourth Gospel* (Harper and Row, New York, 1968).

5. It is probably more correct to regard it as a quotation of Ps. 78.24, adapted in the light of Exod. 16.4. For this point, and for further fascinating details of this brilliant discourse, I must again refer the reader to my forthcoming commentary. Only a fraction of the issues which it raises can be included here.

6. Cf. Matt. 6.9–11: "Our Father who art in heaven . . . give us this day our daily bread" (or "our bread for the morrow"). The meaning of the last phrase (*epiousion*) is uncertain. It is very likely that it means "our bread for the age to come", which in Johannine terms is "our bread of [eternal] life". Hence in the exposition in verses 35–40 the emphasis falls on the permanent efficacy of the gift.

7. See further below, pp. 74f.

8. "The Parable of the Shepherd (John 10.1–5)", in J. A. T. Robinson, *Twelve New Testament Studies* (Studies in Biblical Theology xxxiv) (S.C.M. Press 1962), pp. 67-75.

9. Really the omission of verse 51 requires also the omission of verse 50, as observed by Hartke and followed by Bultmann in the *Ergänzungsheft* of his commentary. Cf. Fortna, p. 187.

10. Against W. Wilkens, "Die Erweckung des Lazarus", *Theologische Zeitschrift* xv (1959), pp. 22–39.

11. Thus the Beloved Disciple is added into the Peter tradition (compare 20.3–10 with Luke 24.12, 34); Mary Magdalene is singled out from the women at the tomb in 20.1f, 11–18; and Thomas is singled out from the apostolic group in 20.19–29. It will be recalled that it is likely that John is not dependent on the Gospel of Luke as we know it, but on sources which Luke has also used independently.

12. "Traces of Thaumaturgic Technique in the Miracles", *Harvard Theological Review* xx (1927), pp. 171-80.

CHAPTER 4

1. See my forthcoming commentary for arguments in support of this view.

2. "John did no Miracle", in *Miracles*, ed. C. F. D. Moule (Mowbrays 1965), pp. 179-202.

3. Cf. the excursus on Pre-existence in R. Schnackenburg, *The Gospel according to St John*, vol. I (Burns & Oates and Herder & Herder, New York, 1968), pp. 494-507.

4. Other "I am" sayings which can be identified as Wisdom invitations are to be found at 6.35; 11.25; 15.1. These belong to sections which I assign to the second edition of the Gospel. Even so the interpretation of them in this way is open to doubt. The same applies to 14.6, which belongs to the first edition. Only by extracting the verse from its context can it be taken in this sense.

5. *JTS* 20 (1969), pp. 41-52.

6. *NTS* 16 (April 1970), pp. 288-95.

7. P. Borgen, *Bread from Heaven* (*Supplements to Novum Testamentum* x) (E. J. Brill, Leiden, 1965).

8. E.g. B. J. Malina, *The Palestinian Manna Tradition* (E. J. Brill, Leiden, 1968); E. E. Ellis, "Midrash, Targum and New Testament Quotations", in *Neotestamentica et Semitica: Studies in Honour of Matthew Black*, ed. M. Wilcox (T. and T. Clark 1969), pp. 61-9.

9. The vexed question of the omission of the institution of the Eucharist from John's Last Supper account cannot be dealt with here. But that John was familiar with the tradition is clear from his use of the eucharistic language in 6.52–8.

10. For the unique feature of a preliminary hearing by Annas I must once more refer the reader to my forthcoming commentary.

SOME BOOKS ON JOHN

Barrett, C. K., *The Gospel according to St John.* S.P.C.K. 1955.

Borgen, P., *Bread from Heaven: An Exegetical Study of the Concept of Manna in the Gospel of John and the Writings of Philo (Supplements to Novum Testamentum* x). Leiden, E. J. Brill, 1965.

Brown, R. E., *The Gospel according to St John* (Anchor Bible Commentary). 2 vols. New York, Doubleday, 1966, 1970 and Geoffrey Chapman 1971.

Bultmann, R., *Das Evangelium des Johannes* (Meyers Kommentar). Göttingen, Vandenhoek & Ruprecht, 1941. English translation: *The Gospel of John.* Basil Blackwell 1971.

Dodd, C. H., *The Interpretation of the Fourth Gospel.* C.U.P. 1953.

—— *Historical Tradition in the Fourth Gospel.* C.U.P. 1963.

Fenton, J. C., *The Gospel according to John* (New Clarendon Bible). Oxford 1970.

Fortna, R. T., *The Gospel of Signs: A Reconstruction of the Narrative Source underlying the Fourth Gospel (Society for New Testament Studies Monograph Series* XI). C.U.P. 1970.

Freed, E. D., *Old Testament Quotations in the Gospel of John (Supplements to Novum Testamentum* XI). Leiden, E. J. Brill, 1965.

Gardner-Smith, P., *St John and the Synoptic Gospels.* C.U.P. 1938.

Higgins, A. J. B., *The Historicity of the Fourth Gospel.* Lutterworth Press 1960.

Hoskyns, E. C., and Davey, F. N., *The Fourth Gospel.* Faber 1947.

Howard, W. F., *Christianity according to St John.* Duckworth 1943.

Hunter, A. M., *According to John.* S.C.M. Press 1968.

Käsemann, E., *The Testament of Jesus* (The New Testament Library). S.C.M. Press 1968.

Lindars, B., *The Gospel of John* (The Century Bible, New Edition). Oliphants (forthcoming).

Marsh, J., *Saint John* (The Pelican Gospel Commentaries). Penguin Books 1968.

Martyn, J. L., *History and Theology in the Fourth Gospel*. New York, Harper & Row, 1968.

Robinson, J. A. T., *Twelve New Testament Studies* (Studies in Biblical Theology XXXIV). S.C.M. Press 1962.

Sanders, J. N., and Mastin, B. A., *The Gospel according to St John* (Black's New Testament Commentaries). Black 1968.

Schnackenburg, R., *The Gospel according to St John*, vol. I. Burns & Oates and New York, Herder & Herder, 1968.

www.ingramcontent.com/pod-product-compliance
Lightning Source LLC
Chambersburg PA
CBHW071107090426
42737CB00013B/2527